CW00392037

MORE MEMORIES OF
HALIFAX

TRUE NORTH BOOKS
DEAN CLOUGH
HALIFAX
HX3 5AX
TEL 01422 344344

THE PUBLISHERS WOULD LIKE TO THANK THE
FOLLOWING COMPANIES FOR SUPPORTING THE
PRODUCTION OF THIS BOOK

MAIN SPONSOR
HALIFAX PLC

BREARLEY GREENS
CALDENE CLOTHING COMPANY LIMITED
CALDERDALE COLLEGE
CALDERDALE METROPOLITAN BOROUGH COUNCIL
CROSSLEY HEATH SCHOOL
JOE DEAN & SONS (HAULAGE) LIMITED
RP DOWSLAND
JAMES FARRAR (BRUSHES) LIMITED
FINN GLEDHILL
FREUDENBERG NONWOVENS L.P.
HALIFAX FAN MANUFACTURING COMPANY LIMITED
HEBDEN CORD COMPANY LIMITED
HOLSET ENGINEERING COMPANY LIMITED
JOHN HORSFALL & SONS (GREETLAND) LIMITED
MCVITIE'S CAKE COMPANY LIMITED
FRED MOORE LIMITED
NESTLÉ UK LIMITED
ERIC L NETHERCOAT LIMITED
NU-SWIFT INTERNATIONAL LIMITED
RICE JONES & SMITHS
HAROLD ROBERTSHAW & SONS LIMITED
SAGAR-RICHARDS LIMITED
S SHEARD & SON LIMITED
ROYAL & SUNALLIANCE INSURANCE COMPANY
R & M SUTCLIFFE LIMITED
ANDY THORNTON ARCHITECTURAL ANTIQUES LIMITED.

First published in Great Britain by True North Books
Dean Clough
Halifax HX3 5AX
1997

All rights reserved. No part of this publication may be reproduced, stored in
a retrieval system, or transmitted in any form, or by any means, electronic,
mechanical, photocopy, recording or otherwise without the prior permission
in writing of the Copyright holders, nor be otherwise circulated in any form
or binding or cover other than in which it is published and without a similar
condition being imposed on the subsequent publisher.

© TRUE NORTH HOLDINGS
ISBN 1 900 463 06 7

Foreword

Halifax is my town. I feel very privileged and honoured to be asked to contribute to *More Memories of Halifax* and play a small part in recording some of the changes which have affected our area, for future generations to read.

The 1950s, '60s and '70s saw us lose some famous names from the textile and engineering industries in Halifax, ranging from Asquiths at Highroadwell to Crossleys Carpets in Dean Clough and, in more recent times we have lost Websters Fountain Head Brewery. Many other businesses went to the wall during some very testing economic times. They are remembered, no doubt, by the countless thousands of Halifax folk who gave them many years of loyal service, for it is people, not machines, buildings or equipment, who make up the character of a company. Jobs may come and go, but they can never take away the skills we have learned at our labours!

As people of Halifax we are fortunate to have many buildings of beauty and interest in our town. The Piece Hall is one of these and it attracts thousands of vistors to see it every year. It reminds us of the days when the sheep farmers and weavers from all over the district would travel to Halifax to sell their wares. Our best-known landmark is at King Cross; Wainhouse Tower was built by a distant relative of my family, a man by the name of Buckley. During the building work, in a terrible accident, a very heavy stone fell on his arm causing it to be amputated. His contribution was still valued however, and he was kept on as Clerk of the Works, overseeing the record-keeping and book-work for the rest of the massive undertaking. My mind is always drawn to the involvement this distant predecessor of mine had in building the tower whenever I drive past it.

Walking through the Borough Market, as I have done many times during my *80-something* years, I am always struck by its beauty, for it is surely one of the most attractive buildings of its kind in the country. I take pride, too, in the achievements of the *Halifax,* once the biggest building society in the world, and now a major bank. This is an institution which reflects well on our town and everyone associated with it. When Crossley Carpets announced that they were to end carpet production in Halifax it was a blow to us all. They were, at one time, our largest employers and based at the historic mills they had built up in Dean Clough. What happened next was remarkable. Praise must go to the great endeavour of Sir Ernest Hall O.B.E who transformed the premises once threatened with decay and dereliction into a leading enterprise and arts centre which is the envy of other towns. New companies, about 150 as I write, have been born out of the ashes of the once mighty carpet manufacturing centre.

It has not all been 'doom and gloom' on the industrial front as far as local companies are concerned. Many of them, thanks to the support of their skilled craftsmen and women, have succeeded in finding customers all over the Britain, and many have taken the name 'Halifax' all over the world. Civic facilities, such as our museums and parks, deserve a mention here too. Halifax has these in abundance and one of the latest jewels in our crown is the Eureka centre which provides entertainment and education for hundreds of thousands of people every year.

In 1973 I had the honour of being asked to open the new by-pass. A major undertaking for the town, it was the culmination of an ambitious project designed to relieve the centre of Halifax from increasing volumes of traffic. The road was named after Alderman Burdock, a hard-working servant of Halifax for many years.

My life in Halifax has been a wonderful experience and I count myself lucky to have been born in such a special place. I have countless happy memories of life with my family, at work and in public service as the last mayor to hold office for a complete year before ' Halifax' became 'Calderdale'. I have enjoyed looking at the pictures which have been selected for this book. Many have rekindled fond memories of the past for me and I feel sure that they will do the same for you. I hope you enjoy reading the book and looking back on how things used to be.

Maurice Jagger
August 1997

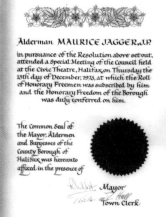

Left: The intricately illustrated certificate that was presented to Maurice Jagger when he became an honourary Freeman of the Borough in 1973

Introduction

The publication of our first local book, *Memories of Halifax,* met with a very pleasing response. Thousands of copies were sold and many found their way to former Halifax residents in different parts of Britain and overseas. Since then we have published around twenty similar books on other northern towns and cities.

Many local companies have allowed us to recount their history through these pages, and fascinating reading it makes too. The businesses are proud of their products and the achievements of their people. Exceptional ingenuity and determination has characterised Halifax industrialists for centuries, and we are pleased to provide a platform for them to share their stories with a wider audience.

The book contains an interesting range of photographs covering a wide time span, but we have concentrated on relatively recent times which should be within the memory of most readers. *Change* is taking place constantly in our town and our sense of perspective inevitably depends on our age and the experiences we have had. As we get older it is usually easier to 'step back' and see events and changes in a clearer light. Our aim has been to provide a catalyst capable of rekindling memories of days gone by in an entertaining manner. During the research for the book many interesting facts have come to light. Of course, the Central Library is full of interesting local facts, contained in a wide range of documents, old newspapers and publications. A lifetime could be spent wading through the material in local libraries and museums, selecting items to create the perfect 'snapshot', for that is all we can do, like a busy shopper wandering up and down the aisles of a well-stocked supermarket.

Our sense of perspective has been made keener as the weeks of research have gone by. Events in a town sometimes appear haphazard, unfocussed and unrelated. The passage of time has allowed us to see things in a rather more sympathetic light. A good example is the change to the 'smokeless' era in Halifax which began in October 1959 and improved our health and the appearance of local buildings dramatically. Reports from the day indicate that the change was not universally welcomed; people complained about the cost and efficiency of alternative fuels and some resisted the zoning of their area under the 'smokeless plan'. The clearance of slum areas, and the damp, insanitary houses which characterised them, was unpopular with many people in the 1960s and early '70s. Housing has always been contentious. In 1960 Halifax had 4,000 dwellings with no hot water, no inside lavatory and no bathroom. The barriers preventing progress have changed over the years:

"Housing is a job nobody wants. Sites are wet and exposed and working on them in the weather we get is difficult. And again, slum clearance plans depend us being able to get the Sanitary Inspectors we need."

These were the words of Alderman Arthur Pickles O.B.E, J.P, Chairman of the Housing Committee, speaking in 1955. At the time 1600 people were waiting on the housing list, and the target was to get the number down to under 1000. Today, finance and philosophy are more likely to prevent British Local Authorities providing the housing people want, not a shortage of tradesmen.

Looking back over the years since the end of the Second War we see a period of tremendous change. Nostalgia often involves a degree of criticism, such as when we look back on the buildings in a town swept away for some new road or shopping centre. We look back with fondness, but forget some of the facts which made the changes inevitable. *We* stopped going to the cinema and theatre in droves when television arrived, and some of us abandoned local shops when we had to walk more than ten yards from our driving seat to get to them; when cars became affordable we all wanted one -and then complained when we couldn't park in the centre of Halifax or had to wait more than two minutes in the rush-hour. Local people demanded solutions - and we got them in the form of multi-storey car parks, shopping centres and relief roads!

Times which don't seem so long ago get a mention in the book if they warrant it. Times as recent as 1970 (when petrol cost just 30p per gallon and the rent in the *new* Shaw Lodge flats was £4. 12s 0d per week) and, where possible, interesting facts have been included from whatever era they originate. An example of this is the fact that Daniel Defoe, author of *Robinson Crusoe,* used to worship at the Northgate End Church where the bus station stands now, and it is said that he began writing his most famous work in a pub on the site of Marks and Spencers. In wartime 1700 local people were prosecuted for breaches of the blackout regulations - resulting in fines of up to £200 per week being collected by the council. The municipal centre of Halifax was once to be found at Union Street, in the days before the present town hall was built..... and so it goes on. These, and other interesting facts will be found in the following pages.

Increasingly, nostalgia is enjoyed by a growing band of enthusiasts and *More Memories of Halifax* is intended to appeal to a wide audience. Compiling the book has been a pleasure and a privilege. We hope you enjoy reading it.

Happy memories!

Phil Holland and Mark Smith, Publishers.

Contents

TEXT
PHIL HOLLAND
PAULINE BELL

DESIGN
MARK SMITH
MANDY WALKER

BUSINESS DEVELOPMENT
GARETH MARTIN

Events and occasions

Left: The end of World War II resulted in celebrations throughout Britain and Halifax was no exception. One of the most memorable changes was the end of the blackout and the abolition of restrictions on lighting, both inside the home and on the streets. The top of Wainhouse Tower was lit up as part of the celebrations to mark the end of the war. Parties were held by scores of local communities and the whole town seemed to be in party mood. Shop windows and streets were festooned with flags and bunting, and, as a national holiday was declared, people began to plan for the future. Obviously, the elation was tinged with sadness; many fine young men would never return to the town and friends and family would have to rebuild their lives without them.

Pictured here are residents of Priestley Place, seen enjoying V.J day with a street party for local children. Rationing and shortages remained well into the 1950s.

Right: Little is known about this picture, save that it is entitled "Smith's Treat' and is one of Gladys Lumb's collection. The area is Northgate and the picture just includes a corner of the area's well-known theatre on the left of the picture. The Grand Theatre and Opera House had a capacity of 2000 people, including 300 standing, and was built at a cost of £16,000. In the early 1950s, the Grand, situated at Northgate, was managed by dedicated band of volunteers and a slim staff of paid stage enthusiasts. The *Grand* was regarded as one of the best venues in the north of England for the quality of its plays and performances. The theatre replaced the *Gaiety* which had stood on the same site.

For all occasions . . .

PRIVATE PARTY OUTINGS

—

TOURS

—

SPORTING EVENTS

—

WEDDINGS ETC.

. . . when you require a coach

CONSULT — *Hebble*

Head Office: WALNUT STREET, HALIFAX. Tel. 2286

—Write or 'phone for our Representative to call upon you—

Left: Coach travel was very popular in the immediate post war years, and would have been the chosen method of holiday-making for those that could afford any kind of holiday at all!

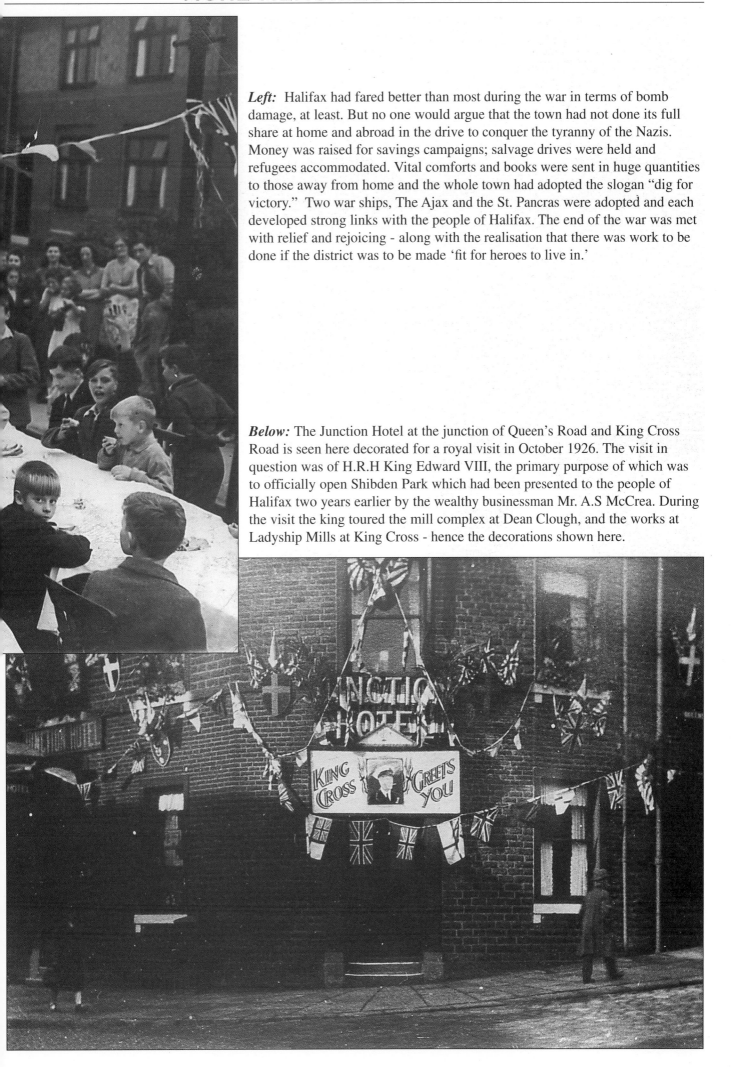

Left: Halifax had fared better than most during the war in terms of bomb damage, at least. But no one would argue that the town had not done its full share at home and abroad in the drive to conquer the tyranny of the Nazis. Money was raised for savings campaigns; salvage drives were held and refugees accommodated. Vital comforts and books were sent in huge quantities to those away from home and the whole town had adopted the slogan "dig for victory." Two war ships, The Ajax and the St. Pancras were adopted and each developed strong links with the people of Halifax. The end of the war was met with relief and rejoicing - along with the realisation that there was work to be done if the district was to be made 'fit for heroes to live in.'

Below: The Junction Hotel at the junction of Queen's Road and King Cross Road is seen here decorated for a royal visit in October 1926. The visit in question was of H.R.H King Edward VIII, the primary purpose of which was to officially open Shibden Park which had been presented to the people of Halifax two years earlier by the wealthy businessman Mr. A.S McCrea. During the visit the king toured the mill complex at Dean Clough, and the works at Ladyship Mills at King Cross - hence the decorations shown here.

Top: "Always take notice of the teacher for the teacher is always right". This was the message from Mayor Sharp J.P when he visited his old school in September 1950. It must have been something of a proud moment for the mayor, an ordinary working man who had climbed the civic ladder to the very top. He told the pupils at Ackroyd Place that 'in his day' there was no organised swimming or sports activity - just an hour's drill each afternoon to keep the children fit and healthy. Mayor Sharp had left the school at the age of 13 to begin work as a part-timer. He recalled that at the time he attended the school there were 1,000 pupils.

Interestingly, the man standing on the right of the Lady Mayoress is Councillor J. Liley, the man who went on to head Liley's pram and toy shop at Cheapside. The children presented the Lady Mayoress with a bouquet of roses to mark the occasion. Sadly, Ackroyd School was demolished in 1969 to make way for the inner relief road scheme.

Above: This thought-provoking photograph from 1952 shows the Mayor and the Lady Mayoress with a group of disabled people who were about to embark upon an annual outing. Hats and coats seemed to be the order of the day. Let's hope that the weather brightened up for the travellers before they arrived at their destination.

Below: "I'm 92 you know..." She was too. It would have been a proud moment for the oldest person on the North Ward old folks treat when she met the Mayor, Alderman Fred Sharp in 1950. Readers may be interested in the outfit worn by the Lady Mayoress, standing on the left of the picture. Furs were worn as something of a status symbol by virtually any lady who could afford them, and if a fur coat was beyond the budget then a stole, either in mink or fox, was the next best thing. The smiles on the faces of the men and women pictured here reflect the popularity of Mayor Sharp; he was an ordinary working man who had worked his way up through the trade union movement in a difficult industry, served on many committees of the council and finally achieved the ultimate in local politics - the honour of being appointed mayor.

Lower picture: The huge sandstone blocks which make up the base of the Town Hall, blackened with decades of pollution from thousands of Halifax chimneys (it was cleaned in 1972), make an almost symbolic backdrop to this picture. *Symbolic* because the well-behaved youngsters standing proudly with the mayor and mayoress of their town had experienced trauma, doubt and uncertainty during their short lives, for they were orphans and their care and protection was the responsibility of the town and its servants.

It is interesting to notice how childrens' fashions have changed since this picture was taken, around half a century ago; the little girls here would not look out of place in a modern setting, but try making your little lad wear a tank top, short trousers and school cap.... let alone a tie!

Above left: The top table at the Hospital Ball in the Victoria Hall in 1950. Mayor Fred Sharp, the Lady Mayoress and other important guests are seen approaching the final lap of their meal and thoughts would, no doubt, be turning to thoughts of speeches cigars and brandy. The party had obviously not let the occasion go to their heads - notice the ever- faithful bottle of H.P sauce in the centre of the table!

Left: A party of ladies about to set off on an outing together. It is known that this was an organised trip from the Prospect Inn at Range Bank to visit a former licensee of the pub who was, by this time, running another establishment in Leeds. The ladies had obviously taken a lot of trouble to dress up for the occasion, looking smart in their summer hats. *The Prospect* is an ideal place to visit for an excellent pint and one of the best views of Halifax.

> **"...PEOPLE LINED THE STREETS TO WATCH THE VARIETY OF INGENIOUSLY CONCEIVED AND PREPARED FLOATS PASS BY."**

Above: Commercial Street in 1965. The occasion is the annual Charity Gala and, as can be seen, the theme for the procession was "Historic Transport". Thousands of people lined the streets to watch the variety of ingeniously conceived vehicles pass by. Commercial Street itself is a thoroughfare steeped in history, dating as it does from about 1880. The construction of this, the main commercial artery through the town, was authorised by the 1853 Improvement Act. It is said that townsfolk originally wanted to call it New South Street, or Oxford Street, but permission for this was turned down. This photograph was taken by someone standing just outside Lloyds Bank, one of the grandest buildings in Halifax. The bank was built in May 1898 and originally opened as the Halifax and Huddersfield Union Banking Company. It became Lloyds Bank in 1919.

Right: A selection of walkers taking part in the Mayor's Procession, probably in the late 1950s or early 1960s. The participants are walking up Crossley Street, away from the direction of the Town Hall. Crossley Street takes its name from John Crossley, of Crossley's Carpets fame, at one time the company had a warehouse in this area, as well as offices located on Crossley Street. The Mechanic's Institute held classes on Crossley Street, before the opening of the Technical College. The building was later to become better known as the local headquarters of the Y.M.C.A. Lloyds Bank had premises here, as did the Halifax Building Society in its very early days, located at the junction of Crossley Street and Princess Street.

Above and facing page: A proud moment for the Mayor of Halifax, Alderman Maurice Jagger J.P, the Lady Mayoress and the rest of the mayoral party assembled for the opening ceremony of the Burdock Way.

The 'Big Walk' as it became known, where the public was encouraged to sample the new route on foot, had taken place the previous Sunday, April 1 1973, and attracted 20,000 participants. Incidentally, April 1st 1973 was the day the V.A.T was introduced in Britain.

This picture was taken on April 6th 1973. The mayoral party had assembled at the King Cross end of the by-pass before travelling across it. The group included Dr Shirley Summerskill, M.P for Halifax and the heads of the firms of consultant engineers and construction contractors who designed and built the roadway. Also in the party was Alderman John Burdock O.B.E, after whom the relief road was named, and Deputy Mayor Coun. George H. Smith, who had the distinction of being the first person to walk upon the newly-opened road.

Within an hour of the road opening there was a noticeable improvement in the flow of traffic through the centre of Halifax, though up to half the normal volume of 'through' traffic was still using the North Bridge route, despite appeals in the local press from the police. The opening of the Burdock Way, the culmination of a dream that was at least 26 years old, was to continue to cause controversy for some time to come. Critics said that the road would 'kill' the centre of Halifax. In the event they were proved wrong, but town centre traders were to face many other challenges in the years that followed.

The birth of home ownership for the many

When the Industrial Revolution further sharpened the rich/poor divide in England, the more philanthropic of the rich mill owners set up the Loyal Georgian Society. Its aim was to lend money to its members to buy their own homes. Unfortunately this society soon ran out of funds and was disbanded. However, one of its members thought of forming a 'permanent' building society instead.

A few already existed in other northern towns, successfully lending the savings of people who had homes to those who had not. 1852 saw the first meeting of the founders of the Halifax Permanent Benefit Building Society at the Old Cock Inn, Halifax. It took place in the Oak Room and the man who recorded the minutes of the proceedings in an old school exercise book could little have dreamed that his society would eventually become the biggest building society in the world.

For a while, headquarters was a shop in Halifax's Old Market, rented for £10 a year. Mr Jonas Dearnley Taylor was appointed as secretary and kept his position for almost half a century. He devoted his life to making home ownership a possibility for as many people as possible.

Sir Enoch Hill

Business burgeoned quickly. In 1853 the first subscription meeting was held. A subscription was expected from both investors and borrowers as a regular instalment towards a share in the society. In 1862 the first branch opened in Huddersfield and by 1863 the society had to restrict the number of mortgages for the first, but not the last time, because of high interest rates and an increase in the demand for loans. By 1885, the Halifax had the largest reserves of all the Yorkshire building societies. In 1888 'paid up shares' were offered for the first time to investing members who

had completed payment on their subscription shares and who wanted to continue their membership.

By 1905 the Halifax had more accounts than any other building society and by 1913 their assets exceeded £3 million - more than any other society. In 1913, by coincidence, the second largest building society was also situated in Halifax and it seemed logical therefore that the two societies should merge. In combination the two societies would be invincible. And so in 1928, the Halifax Permanent Benefit Building Society and the Halifax Equitable merged to form the Halifax Permanent Building Society. With assets of £47 million it was five times larger then its nearest rival.

In the early days, the society employed men to work for them as agents in the areas where they lived. They called at people's homes to collect funds. By the late 1890's, the

agents all had offices where customers brought business to them. There were 50 of these agencies by 1903 when, on the death of Mr Jonas Taylor, Mr Enoch Hill became the new secretary. Mr Hill was a driving force behind the society's expansion and whenever a new branch opened he made it a special occasion, with a party and important local people as guests. Celebrations were particularly extravagant when the first Halifax Office opened in London.

Continued overleaf.

Facing page, top: Permanent buildings, the former head office of the Halifax Building Society. Built in 1921, this picture dates from the 1940s. ***Far left:*** *Sir Enoch Hill, the man credited with masterminding the society's expansion in the early part of this century.* ***Left:*** *Wartime saw the head office shrouded in this blast wall as a precaution against air raids.* ***Above:*** *The outline of this building site, captured in a 1970 aerial photograph, provides a clue to the design influences that shaped the thinking of the new head office.*

On the 50th anniversary of this particular opening, the society was invited to take part in the Lord Mayor of London's parade. The theme that year was 'children' so the Halifax had a float based on nursery rhyme characters. Staff working in the society's City Offices made their own costumes. The text of the various nursery rhymes decorated the float, the words slightly changed to illustrate the benefits of being a member of the Halifax! Nowadays, new offices are opened without so much fuss. Enoch Hill, however, was knighted for his sterling efforts, original ideas and other services to the society. More recently, Jim Birrell, Halifax Chief Executive in the late 1980s and early 1990s was also knighted in

recognition of his efforts to promote home ownership in the UK.

Time for a move

The headquarters in Commercial Street served the Halifax well for over 50 years and during this time assets rose to over £3 billion. However more space was required and the present site of the so-called diamond shape building in Trinity Road became available. Work began in 1969 on the old Ramsdens Brewery site and the society moved in in 1973. The new head office was officially opened by Her Majesty the Queen in the following year. The new building, rising above a shopping street won various design awards, but at the time some local people were not impressed. It did not, they claimed, fit in with the Victorian buildings that surrounded it. However, over time, most doubters come round to it as it became more familiar and it is now widely viewed as a building ahead of its time and has become a well-known landmark which dominates the Halifax skyline.

The Head office site contains many surprises and indeed

there is as much space below ground as there is above. A huge vault, nearly 50 feet below street level is known as Deed Safe and contains all the title deeds to the properties bought with a Halifax mortgage. Title deeds to over one fifth of the UKs housing market are stored, encased in concrete and protected by the latest safety and security devices. The filing is nowadays done by computer and the vault is linked to the Deeds Department three floors above the ground by bright red conveyors which turn like helter skelters and deliver, in a moving column, deeds required by staff. There is capacity for almost three million packets of title deeds in the vault so a new vault will not be required in the immediate future.

In 1988, the Head Office complex was extended still further when a new six-floor office block was built on the site of the former Collinsons tea and coffee warehouse at the side of the diamond shaped building. Again the building won various design awards for the innovative and sympathetic way it was incorporated into the local environment.

Copley

The Halifax has been at the forefront of new Technology for a number a years and it was decided in the 1980s that it needed a purpose built data centre so that it could enter the *Continued overleaf*

Facing page, top: This 1920s picture of the counter area in the head office is in marked contrast to the modern, relaxed layout of today's typical Halifax branch. **Left:** *The computer building, shown here under construction in 1976, marked the beginning of the development of the area to the rear of what was then the Ramsdens brewery premises, later to become the site of the diamond shaped head office building.* **Above:** *The sheer scale of the engineering undertaking involved in the spectacular design of the new head office is captured in this early 1970s photograph, taken from the side of the ABC cinema.* **Below:** *The Leeds Permanent building society head office on The Headrow, circa 1930. The merger of two societies in 1995 paved the way for the subsequent flotation.*

1990s and the new millennium with confidence. The purpose built centre, on the outskirts of Halifax, on the site of an old rhubarb field, ensures a continuous supply of computer power and expertise to utilise it. It houses the central processors and digital communications equipment. Built in 1989, there are back-up facilities, off-site, capable of taking over if any problems should occur. The computer systems operate in an IBM environment but actual computer equipment is from a variety of manufacturers. At any one time the centre will control over 30,000 workstations throughout the Halifax's branch network as well as having telecommunication links with almost every country in the world. Halifax, once viewed as the centre of mechanical expertise due to the textile trade, is now quite rightly viewed as one of the leading centres of Information Technology in the UK.

During the 1980s the expansion of the organisation continued at pace. In 1980, the Halifax gave its one millionth mortgage and its assets topped £10 billion. In 1996 the Halifax had 20 million accounts and its assets exceeded £115 billion.

Merger with the Leeds

Building Societies have had to change and adapt due to the increased competition, mainly from the banks. Customers have started to demand a wider range of products and services and the Halifax has usually been at the forefront of new product design and innovation. It now offers a vast range of products and raises funds not only through its traditional avenues of retail savings accounts, but also through the wholesale money markets. The Halifax Treasury Department, based in Halifax, raises funds in the money markets of London, Europe, America and Asia and its computerised and hi-tech equipment is the envy of many London based dealing rooms.

In November 1994, the Halifax made the historic announcement that it was to merge with the Leeds Permanent Building Society (then the 5th largest building society) and then to convert to a public limited company, Not only did this involve the biggest building society merger in UK history but it was then followed by the largest extension of Share ownership ever witnessed in the UK. The whole process was a gigantic logistical operation which was masterminded by a small team in Halifax but ably supported by the help of the thousands of Halifax staff throughout the country. The merger of the two

organisations took place an Yorkshire Day, 1 st August 1995, and then the conversion to plc on 2nd June 1997. Over 7.5 million Halifax members became shareholders and the organisation became the 8th largest company in the UK.

The new Halifax offers an extensive range of products and services, ranging from savings schemes for children, a comprehensive range of banking products as well as a range of savings accounts for people of all ages, both on and offshore. The Halifax continues to be the UK's largest mortgage lender and has recently been awarded the coveted title of 'lender of the decade' by a specialist financial publication.

The future

Like all successful organisations, the Halifax plans to become both bigger and better. It realises it can never stay still and it continues to look towards the future. It is continuing to develop its services to its mainland customers, but also developing its offshore activities in Jersey and the Isle of Man which act as bases for British expatriates. The Halifax is looking to extend its services in other European markets and its Spanish subsidiary, Banco Halifax Hispania, based in Madrid, Seville and Barcelona, is evidence of this. The Halifax also participates in the European Community Mortgage Federation, helping in the development of legislation to create an effective single European market for housing.

And of course, to Halifax residents, the presence of one of the UKs top ten companies in our own town centre will continue to be a source of pride and employment well into the next millennium.

Above: This recent aerial picture of the northern side of Halifax town centre provides an unusual perspective on the diamond shaped head office building. The landscaped roof gardens are one of the less well known features and the glass side extension on the left hand side of the picture is also clearly visible.

Victorian values with a 21st century approach

Calderdale College celebrated a century of educational achievement in 1993 and at the same time it became independent of local authority control. These two events were very significant in the development of the college.

The origins of Calderdale College lay in an initiative by local politicians, companies and the Halifax Mechanics Institute to develop a 'technical school' to meet the education and training needs of the local economy and community. From the very beginning the college has been a partnership, with local employers and community organisations playing a prominent part on the governing body and influencing its teaching. Local companies and benefactors subscribed to the original funds and provided equipment for the college; the Halifax Incorporated Chamber of Commerce

Calderdale College valued its highly accomplished musicians. This picture of a music group dates from the 1950s.

A 1950s bricklaying course. The building trade during this period was a 'safe' industry as new houses were being built all over the country.

contributed to the development of the Commercial Education Scheme, set examinations and offered prizes to successful students in the 1890s.

Today the new governing body of the Calderdale Colleges Corporation is drawn from the local business community and a vital part of its mission is to respond effectively to training demands. It is an aim that the Victorian founders of the college would have understood. As a speaker at the opening of the college in 1893 put it: "Industries are in a constant state of transition owing to new

discoveries and new initiatives, and we need people who can take advantage of all the changes which our industries are undergoing and who have the necessary flexibility and elasticity of mind...." Quite!

By modern standards the College was small. In 1896 it consisted of one laboratory, a weaving shed and a number of classrooms with one full- time and twenty three part-time teachers who taught around 1000 students. Today the Calderdale Colleges Corporation teaches over 13,000 students throughout Calderdale. The Corporation now consists of; Calderdale College (made up of the Schools of Administration and Computing; Management; Health, Care and Education; Customer Services; Foundation Studies); Halifax New College (the Corporation's 6th Form College); Halifax School of Integrated Arts (combining art, design, performing arts, crafts and construction); Local Learning (the Corporation's Community Education Programme) and Calderdale Associates Ltd (a managing agent with Calderdale & Kirklees Training and Enterprise Council).

This picture of the domestic staff dates from the 1950s.

Despite a hundred years of change in Calderdale there are elements of continuity showing the college's strong and close links with local business and the community.

In the 1890s it was possible to take external degrees from the University of London. Continuing this tradition,

The start of 'A mile of pennies' beginning in Woolshops in the 1950s. Percival Whitley can be seen far left watching the events.

Calderdale College launched a part time degree programme in the early 1990s in conjunction with the University of Huddersfield.

As an essential part of the community the college shared in all the major successes and trials faced by Calderdale people. Members of the staff and former students fought in the two world wars and the college made a contribution to the war effort by training engineering workers for war work, teaching food supply and organisation for the Ministry of Supply and running courses in army organisation for the ATS. At the conclusion of both wars the college was involved with rehabilitation and retraining programme for demobilised service personnel.

The Calderdale Colleges Corporation's roots lie in the self improvement tradition of the nineteenth century and the Victorian ideal of service to the community. Building on this tradition, the modern Calderdale Colleges have developed programmes to broaden educational opportunities ranging from part time degree courses through to retraining and upskilling of women returning to work and for unemployed people looking for a new direction. It now has extensive European Community support as well as government and industry funding.

For much of the century education and training was linked to Calderdale's traditional industries of engineering and textiles. As new industries have developed the Calderdale Colleges have responded to

these changes by broadening services to cover new technologies and skills.

As the Calderdale Colleges Corporation looks forward to the next century, it is keen to build on the strengths and traditions of the past. Training and education of the highest quality are going to be more important in the future development of Britain's economy.

Just as our Victorian forebears recognised the value of quality education and training to enable local companies and workers to meet the challenges of a new century, so the Calderdale Colleges Corporation sees itself as central to the development of the local economy of Calderdale in the years ahead.

Percival Whitley in Bull Green announcing that Ajax has beaten the National fund-raising record for Warships Week in 1942.

The Halifax 'Heritage Trail'

❝From Hell, Hull and Halifax, Good Lord deliver us'. This northern addition to the Litany, was a reaction to the two towns' singularly harsh methods of proceeding against thieves that struck terror in vagabonds throughout Yorkshire. As the north-south divide developed, however, the expression has been quoted, most unfairly, as evidence of the hostile environment in the industrial north. Any visitor to Halifax will find much scenery that is pleasing to the eye and plenty of interesting things to do and see, many of which have been provided by the Calderdale MBC.

Shibden Hall

The Good Weekend Guide for 1995 named this 15th century house among Britain's 50 most enjoyable museums outside London.
This black and white timbered hall, surrounded by its 90 acre park, is owned by Calderdale Borough Council. It was built in around 1420 and occupied first by the Otes family and then the Saviles and Waterhouses until Samuel Lister became the tenant in about 1614. With the marriage of his son Thomas, in 1619, to one of the heiresses of Shibden Hall, it came into the ownership of the notable diarist, traveller, communicator and lesbian, Anne Lister, who extended and modernised it.

In the early 20th century, Shibden Hall was the home of the antiquarian John Lister. Following his death, the Hall passed to local authority ownership and opened as a

A postcard dating from the early 1900s, showing the many facets of Shibden Hall.

museum on 4 June 1934. The house is completely furnished, its most famous displays being the collection of 17th century Yorkshire oak furniture. Its rooms include a kitchen, the housebody or hall parlour, study, bed chambers and powder closet. In the nearby Pennine barn, built c1670, are early agricultural implements - ploughs, peat-spades, hay knives, threshing machine and other tools of a farmer of 100 years ago. The dairy, with its stone floor, cheese press, churns and cream troughs, is ready for making butter and cheese.

A magnificent series of horse-drawn vehicles - from the Lister chaise dating from about 1750 to a barouche, and including a State Chariot, a World War I ambulance and a gypsy vardo - stand in the barn. Beyond this is a brewhouse with large vat, wooden troughs and lead and copper pumps still capable of making strong ale. Craft workshops surround the courtyard, each giving the impression that its craftsman has just nipped out to lunch leaving his tools where he was using them. Here you will find a wheelwright, blacksmith, cooper, clogger and saddler. There is also a pub, the fittings of the Crispin Inn of Luddite fame, and a cottage where you will see the utensils to make our local oatbread, called havercakes.

Throughout its nine month season, there is a series of special events held in the Hall. An innovative education programme has been developed and visitors may be fortunate enough to glimpse some of Shibden's previous residents explaining life here in days gone by.

Heptonstall Museum

In 1642, Thomas Greenwood founded a grammar school for the boys of yeoman clothiers to be educated in Latin and algebra. The school closed early in the 20th century and then later opened as a branch of Yorkshire Penny Bank. The grammar school was offered by the

Shibden Hall - the housebody

The entrance to Heptonstall Grammar School.

Yorkshire Penny Bank to Hepton Rural District Council on a no cost basis in 1954, when bank business was transferred to Hebden Bridge.

The original flagged floor can still be seen, as can two of the school desks carved with pupils' initials and the schoolmasters desk, with text books recording long forgotten lessons.

The museum's displays reflect the history of the Upper Calder Valley, a close-knit community where the Cragg Vale Coiners were able to counterfeit gold currency in the 18th century. In the 19th century, fustian and

Bankfield Lodge, the entrance to the museum circa 1920

corduroy were woven locally and finished with long knives. Heptonstall was a thriving hilltop township dominated by both the Church and the Methodist Chapel. Local law and order was maintained by an exclusively male Prosecution Society and the museum houses their beautiful silver ceremonial maces.

Bankfield Museum

From 1837 to 1856, the mansion was the residence of Colonel Edward Akroyd, the largest wool manufacturer in Britain. He lavished money and attention on the building, transforming it from a modest town house into a magnificent ltalianate mansion with elaborate painted frescoes, ceilings and plasterwork.

Bankfield Museum, Boothtown has always been a popular destination for vistors to Halifax.

Around Bankfield he built Akroyden, a model village of fine terraced houses with allotments, a park, co-operative store, stables and All Souls Church. It was to be the first 'Urban Village'.

The house was bought by the Council in 1887 for £6,500 for use as a public art gallery, museum and park. Bankfield is now home to an internationally important collection of textiles and costumes from around the world. Mummy wrapping and teddy bears; a Diaghilev ballet costume and lgbo masquerade dress- embroideries from India and China and woven cloth from Africa and Burma all have a place in this 'World of Textiles'. The museum has for many years also been proud home to The Duke of Wellington's Regimental Museum with displays of mementoes from the early 1700s belonging to the Iron Duke to material collected by the Regiment whilst on tour in Bosnia.

Not everything at Bankfield is old. Contemporary crafts are an important part of its permanent galleries and there is a varied and exciting programme of temporary exhibitions, workshops, seminars, master classes and gallery demonstrations.

The site of the Calderdale Industrial Museum seen when it still housed Stirk engineering company.

Calderdale Industrial Museum

This museum is housed in a former engineering factory and tells 'Ripping Yarns', tales of change about lives and livelihoods at the dawn of the factory age. It has working machinery, a children's play area with special activity sessions, workshops for teachers and public lectures amongst the attractions on offer. It was opened in 1985, one of the most comprehensive and innovative industrial museums in the country. In 1993, possibly because of the innovations at EUREKA!, people's perceptions were changing. Traditional labelling of objects on display was found boring. Though they had always been proud that 'nothing is picked in aspic', the staff invested in the fashionable 'hands on' way of finding out for oneself. A Timeline now leads visitors back to the 1930s and sets memories working with sounds and smells, a steam train leaving a station, the smell of fish and chips frying, the sound of Henry Hall's music on the radio. The new

approach had the museum shortlisted for an award from the Gulbenkian Foundation. Visitors leave the 20th century at the door and become time travellers. In the basement, they find the local history of mines and quarrying, engineering and machine tools.

The ground floor offers a 'power sources' display, a shop and exhibition area. The first floor entitled 'Made in Calderdale' tells the story of the many products manufactured here, including 'Cat's Eyes', skips, rope, cork, carpets, toffee and washing machines! It also tells the story of the Halifax Building Society. Halifax in the 1850s lives on the second floor, together with early textile machinery. One of the star attractions is the original blade from the Halifax gibbet.

Those fascinated by machinery and engines can also obtain special information packs and talk to engineers who have had experience of working in textile mills.

Piece Hall Art Gallery

From the Industrial Museum and Piece Hall itself, there is free admission to the Piece Hall Art Gallery with its lively programme of temporary exhibitions and educational activities. Visitors can learn new skills and have fun on monthly art and craft activity days and meet the artist sessions which are advertised in the local press and free Museums and Arts News. There is also a popular Saturday Art Club for children.

The Smith Art Gallery

The gallery in Brighouse is housed, together with the town Library, in a late 18th century house, the gift of the

The Smith Art Gallery in Brighouse in 1907

first Mayor of Brighouse - Alderman William Smith. He became mayor in 1893, but began his art collection in the 1870s. The collection is very typical of the type of sentimental art favoured during the late Victorian period. It is

The opening of the Victoria Theatre took place in 1910. Here, the foundation stones are just being laid.

nevertheless very charming and contains some high quality works by leading artists such as Atkinson Grimshaw's 'Mossy Glen' and Marcus Stone's 'Silent Pleading'. During refurbishment in 1990, the gallery was returned to its original colour scheme of 'Pompeian Red' and original benches, which were rediscovered at Shibden Hall, have been reinstated. In addition to the permanent collection, the gallery has a temporary exhibition programme and education activities, including, for example, popular print and collage workshops for children.

The Halifax Victoria Theatre

In 1897, a group of Halifax citizens banded together under the explicit if rather cumbersome title, 'The Concert Hall and Public Rooms Company Limited', to buy the site at Wards End. They were tired of waiting for public officials to purchase a concert hall for the town and, between them managed to put together the necessary £8,169. The hall was opened with a concert given by the Halifax Choral Society, but all the gentry of Halifax attended the grand official opening in 1901 when a concert was given by the Halle Orchestra. It was the realisation of the town's hopes and dreams. The Halle's

conductor, Hans Richter, asked for his hearty congratulations to be conveyed to the architect, which says something for the hall's acoustic.

The great organ, donated by Miss Elizabeth Porter in September 1901 cost more than £3,000. At its public presentation a recital was given by Dr. J. Kendrick Pyne and the entire proceeds from the performance were donated to the Royal Halifax Infirmary fund.
In May 1960 the building was bought by the Corporation for £82,000. It was never completely closed during the succeeding modernisation and renovation. After this £200,000 face-lift, there was a civic reopening in January 1964 with a celebration lunch and speeches from the Mayor of Halifax, Alderman W. Haigh and from Viscount Mackintosh. The old water-powered organ , which had also been modernised, was played on this occasion by Mr. Shackleton Pollard.

The stage and backstage accommodation had been rebuilt, seats replaced, and refreshment bars provided.

This postcard would have been sent to friends and family of people visiting Halifax at the turn of the century.

The refurbished building was to be used for civic functions, amateur and professional stage productions, dinners, and dances. Appropriately, the first concert after the renovation was again given by the Halle Orchestra.
In 1993 the Civic Theatre became the Victoria Theatre. With its change of name came a change of image. Now professional pantomime companies, ballet companies, touring theatre companies and symphony orchestras perform at the 'Vic' alongside local music and drama groups.

A slightly different view of the Victoria Theatre, dating from a similar period to the picture above.

Around the town centre

Right: Bull Green, the name thought to have been derived from its function as a cattle market or possibly a place where bulls were once baited by dogs in the sixteenth century, is one of the best known areas of Halifax.

The area around Bull Green underwent its biggest change with the opening of Bull Green House complete with garden forecourt layout, in June 1932. In the years before the Bull Green House plan was approved many other schemes, including proposals for an art gallery, swimming baths and a bus station were considered. Dozens of old and dilapidated buildings packed this gateway to the town which now seems so pleasantly open and airy. 1924 saw the Corporation advertise for tenders for the clearance of this property and a year after that saw the completion of shops along King Cross Street which represented the first stage of the project. The cost by modern standards seems modest; £32,000 for business compensation and land clearance, and just £26,000 for the building work.

In 1966 plans were submitted for the construction of a multi-storey car park with a garage beneath it by Ralph Hardy & Co. The completed building later housed the Comet electrical store for many years until they moved into their out-of-town retail park at Pellon Lane.

Below: The junction of Broad Street and Waterhouse Street showing a rare view of Halifax's Wesley Chapel on the right of the picture. It was built in 1829 and closed in 1949. The building was pulled down in the 1960s.

Left: Long before the days of traffic lights and pedestrian sub-ways, this scene was captured at the junction of Cow Green and Pellon Lane. This was once an extremely busy road junction, and was generally only made workable by a point-duty police officer working hard to keep the traffic flowing. This is a 1940s photograph, dominated by the imposing presence of the Grand Junction Hotel on the left, and Ebenezer Church on the right. The Grand Junction stood on Swine Market from its opening in 1864, just a year after the Town Hall had been opened by Edward VII, until it was closed in January 1968. The building was later demolished. The photographer was standing a little way down Central Street when he took the photograph. Atmosphere is given to the scene by the presence of the soldier about to cross Cow Green. We shall never know who he was or where he was going, let alone what the following turbulent years would bring for him.

Below: An autumn day over half a century ago, in a photograph featuring the top of George Street as we have rarely seen it. The area on the right hand side of the view is Barum Top and the dark building displays the sign 'Typewriting' and contains the tobacconist's shop run by Churchill Smith. The typewriting service was offered, with a shorthand facility, by the enterprising Nora Hellowell. You may just be able to read a sign in the window of the public house on the right, identifying it as the Griffin Hotel. Across the way we see the old Bull's Head pub and, following that, the premises of F.C Cooke the newsagents and Seed Bros. the 'boot and shoe dealers'. Tram cables are much in evidence, as is a lovely ornamental street lamp on the traffic island in the foreground. A discreet sign on the lamp post politely directs motorists 'to the municipal car park'. The 'island' of characterful buildings on the left of the picture were pulled down shortly after this scene was captured, to be replaced by the new Bull's Head and a wider, more accessible George Street.

Left: This view will be unfamiliar to all but the very oldest readers. It features a row of commercial properties at the top of George Street, with Barum Top on the right hand side of the picture. The Bull's Head is the building on the right, it is of course the *old* Bull's Head, the *new* one being constructed in August 1940. Overhead tram cables can be seen in this photograph, further confirmation that this picture dates from the 1930s. The road can be seen here sweeping to the right, down Silver Street. Many, but certainly not all of the changes which affected Halifax were related to transportation in general, and the growth in car ownership in particular. Numbers had risen greatly since the turn of the century; in 1901 there were fewer than a dozen motorcars on the roads of Halifax. The registration number 'CP 1' was first used from December 21 1903. By 1955 there were just over 4000 private cars registered in the borough.

Above: Roadworks at Bull Green would have meant an additional headache for the point-duty policeman seen on the right of this picture. In the days before traffic lights and traffic wardens the control of traffic was a major element of police work. Policemen would often work at the same junction and become local personalities, known to regular travellers on a particular route. It often surprises people to learn that the level of road accidents in the 1930s, '40s and '50s was much higher than we experience today, despite the fact that modern volumes of traffic are very much larger. There are several interesting aspects of this scene which are worth a mention, not least of which being the wartime air-raid siren on the top of Bull Green House. The bus shelter behind the lorry has long disappeared and a large roundabout has replaced the once neatly arranged cobble stones. Arthur Farrar's shop at Bull Green House stands across the way from Woodhead and Co., the toy shop being studied in the picture by a young family. Perhaps someone was about to take ownership of their first bicycle?

Left: Extensive clearance of property along Northgate was taking place in this rare photograph from the 1940s. The site was eventually to become dominated by the new Council Offices and Central Library, though this would not take place until the 1970s. This area was the subject of much development in relatively recent years. The area between Woolshops and Wade Street contained some of the town's oldest and most dilapidated property, a warren of run down workshops and crumbling warehouses in a network of dark alleyways.

Below left: The flats along King Cross Street, located just above the 'Courier offices, on the same side of the road, were built in 1934-5. They stood here, between King Cross Street and West Parade in two blocks of 18 flats, with steps and balconies at the rear leading to the upper storey. the design of the flats was unusual in as much as they incorporated small ground floor recesses opening out onto the main road. they were too small to be of any practical use and residents often complained that they served only to attract litter and the occasional person sheltering from the rain.

The Playhouse, is just around the corner from this view.

Formerly the Chapel of the Methodist New Connexion, and built in 1835, the Playhouse was once under threat of demolition. It opened as the *Playhouse* on King Cross Road in September 1949, exactly 22 years to the day after the Halifax Thespians had been founded at the White Swan.

"Smoke from the electricity power station fills the air of Halifax with pollution. There is no place in this county that requires more serious effort to implement this Clean Air Act than Halifax" So said a visiting councillor from Leeds when asked to comment on the efforts being made in the town to comply with the newly imposed regulations to combat air pollution.

The first smokeless zone was introduced in Halifax in October 1959 in accordance with the 1956 Clean Air Act. It covered the very centre of the town, the boundaries being Union Street, Market Street, Northgate, Broad Street, New Broad Street, Cow Green, Lister Lane, the westerly boundary of the New Brunswick Street development area, Hopwood Lane, Bull Green, Barum Top, Fountain Street and Horton Street. September 1961 would see the introduction of smokeless zones at Mixenden and in the Skircoat area.

The pages of the Evening Courier gave prominent coverage to the feelings of local householders who compared the benefits of the new smokeless fuel with the coal they had previously been used to. Some complained that they could no longer burn their household rubbish under the new smokeless rules, and even worse, that the new fuel was more expensive and didn't last as long. The smokeless fuel was priced at 10s 7d per bag and coke at 8s 11d in 1959. Officials worked out that the first three months of the smokeless era saw Halifax burn 200 tons *less* of the soft coal which was associated with the worst pollution. Mixenden was to be the next area on the hit list of the smoke busters - 1189 houses in the 365 acre district.

Below: The domination of the tramway era can be detected in this photograph, with a mass of slippery cold tramlines underfoot and a spiders' web of overhead cables carrying the sparking current for the clattering cars. The view was captured on Fountain Street, looking in the direction of Bull Green. The picture is around sixty years old and is fairly unusual in as much as it clearly shows a young lady driving the cute little motorcar towards Ward's End. Behind the vehicle we see no less than seven industrial chimneys on the skyline, as well as a clear view of the Crown and Anchor. On the right, in the property which would later become the location of various 'themed' public houses, a gentleman's club, with a small number of rooms for overnight accommodation, was based.

Right: This sweeping corner at the bottom of Broad Street, joining Northgate, has changed little since this late 1950s picture was taken, though the buildings around it have changed beyond recognition. The premises of the Midland Mail Order Co. and the Unitarian Church were demolished in 1982. The zebra crossings in the picture have been replaced by Pelican Crossings.

The first such crossing in Halifax was introduced at Godley Bank in March 1976. A ceremony was arranged to formally open it, the honour going to County Councillor Tom Lawler. The occasion turned out to be something of an embarrassment, for on the third change of the lights an unsuspecting motorist failed to stop and ran his car into the back of a lorry, putting the lights out of action and causing several red faces in the process.

Left: Take a moment or two to study this photograph and consider what the area looks like today. Only one building in the scene remains at the time of writing, and there has been talk recently of removing that to make way for the latest retailing brainwave. The Star Hotel is the building in question, standing around the corner from the Odeon, on Orange Street. This photograph dates from the 1940s and is given additional character by the different motor vehicles in the scene.

Below: A photograph dating from 1938, showing construction work in progress on Commercial Street as yet another cinema is born. The cinema in question is the *Regal* later to become known as the A.B.C and later still the Cannon. Ward's End and the surrounding streets developed into the entertainment centre of the town. At one time there was seating for almost 10,000 people within a stones' throw of each other. When it opened, in September 1938, the Regal alone could seat over 1900 people. By 1961 the name change to A.B.C had taken place, and by 1976 it had been converted into three cinemas, following the trend of offering more choice to attract an ever dwindling audience.

This is a rather unusual photograph as it shows work in progress on such a large section of land in the town centre. The land was formerly a plot used by the Hebble Motor Company. It is interesting to see the large number of advertising boards surrounding the building site and the products of the day which were being promoted. In recent times there has been a welcome resurgence in the popularity of *cinema* and the future of the ABC looks assured.

Right: Nostalgia buffs will remember the old fire station located a little way up Gibbet Street. The fire station had been built on the site of the first Halifax cattle market to be run on a purpose-built plot. It is likely that the old building would have become obsolete before much longer in any case, but the needs of the new inner relief road meant that the property had to come down. Older readers may be able to remember the public house opposite the old fire station, the Corporation Arms; it too was cleared in the redevelopment programme. The new fire station in King Cross was opened, after many delays, in 1970. At £225,000, it cost rather more than the Gibbet Street property it replaced.

Left: A view across the rooftops of Halifax from just above the yard of St. Joseph's School. The years after the end of the second world war saw an emphasis on improving the housing stock and general sanitary conditions in the area. The drive was typical of most towns in the country and was encouraged by the government of the day. Improvements to housing formed part of the generally increasing awareness of public health issues and the importance of healthier living.

During 1955 there were 1600 people on Halifax's housing waiting list. An ambitious corporation house building programme sought to build around 400 houses per year. The Corporation did not always find it easy to reach its housing target. Labour shortages were one reason, materials shortages another; costs were under great scrutiny and a variety of construction styles were tried, such as pre-fabricated houses and bungalows, in order to reduce the cost of each dwelling.

Speaking in 1955, Alderman Arthur Pickles O.B.E J.P said "Housing is a job nobody wants. Sites are wet and exposed, and working on them in the weather we get is difficult. And again, slum clearance plans depend upon us being able to get the inspectors we need".

Plans for new housing were closely linked to slum clearance programmes, for obvious reasons.

Reports from 1965 described how the town had 4000 houses which lacked hot water and inside toilets. There were 6000 houses in the town's clearance and redevelopment programme which was scheduled to be completed by 1972, at a rate of 772 properties per year.

Below: An elevated view from high above Dean Clough, looking across the rooftops towards Halifax town centre. Much of the property in the foreground has been cleared since the picture was taken. The property on the left, in the Cross Hills area beside North Bridge, was the subject of much controversy and often blamed for giving the approaches to the town a very run-down appearance. There are gaps in the properties along the roadside which are visible here, for demolition work and a general drive to upgrade the area had already begun. The modern high-rise property on the right is the newly-built Albion Court Flats. Halifax was about to undergo many changes over the coming years; changes which, like the building of the dramatic overhead roadway which would later dominate this scene, would require the demolition of her oldest and most familiar buildings.

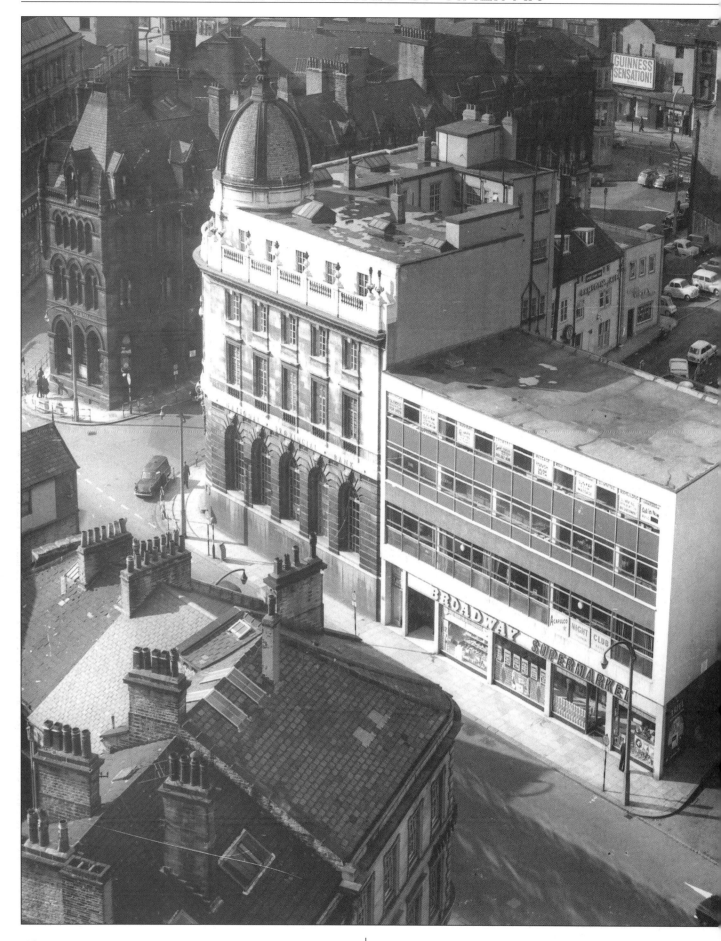

Above: A rare elevated view of Waterhouse Street and the land beyond, showing the premises of the Yorkshire Bank and the Broadway Supermarket. The triangle of open land towards the top of the picture was used as a car park before the block of offices known as Crown House, and the shops and nightclub running along Broad Street were built. Crown House now dominates the skyscape at the top of Broad Street, with its modern office accommodation on nine floors. The building of Crown House and the adjacent modern shops and nightclub premises took place in 1968 and was completed at a cost of £250,000. The former Crossfield bus station is just visible on the right of this

noramic view, which provided the travellers of Halifax with od service for over thirty years, until the new bus station on rthgate took its place. Government offices have since been lt on the site.

other landmark in this view is the Grand Junction Hotel, its ckened stonework can be seen on the corner of Cow Green and Pellon Lane - an area known as Swinemarket. The hotel was demolished in 1968 to be replaced by the concrete and brick hostelry initially named the "Pot o' Four", today known as "Hangovers", perhaps because of its top-heavy architecture - or maybe for another reason altogether!

Now taken for granted, these and other high-rise dwellings have a social significance which goes unnoticed by most people. This pair of tower blocks is only a stones' throw away from one of *old* Halifax's most insanitary areas of housing, described in detail elsewhere in this book and known as 'The City'. The age of the *high-rise* has been criticised by many, and it is true that some developments have not served their residents well. The other side of the coin is that, in their early years, these blocks gave many of their tenants their first experience of inside toilets, bathrooms and hot water, and got them away from conditions which made them ill and reduced the life expectancy of their families. The Shaw Lodge flats were opened at the other end of town in 1970. Many former residents of King Cross were re-housed there at rents of £3.11s 1d for a single bedroomed flat and £4.12s 0d for the two bedroomed version.

Above: Crosshills, the area near the 'town-centre' end of North Bridge during the construction of an elevated section of Halifax's inner relief road. This photograph was taken by Gladys Lumb, and is one of many in this book taken by the well-known local lady over many years and, since her passing, held in the extensive collection treasured by Stephen Gee.
Work is in progress here over the busy road to Illingworth and Keighley, some of the most ambitious and dramatic civil engineering work that our town has ever seen.

Left: The building at the bottom left of this photograph is the Odeon, once a cinema and now, of course, a bingo club. This is the busy junction of Broad Street and Orange Street in a scene dating from the 1960s. The Albion Court and St. James's Court flats are the main features on this picture.

Top: What a difference stone cleaning was to make to the character of the town when it peeled away decades of sooty deposits which had clung to our victorian buildings. In February 1970 properties at the junction of Northgate and Broad Street were identified for demolition because of the outward movement of their walls. They are pictured here, right on the edge of the junction, where now stands a small car park.
Demolition work cost £4,000 and reports said that repairs would have amounted to just over twice that sum. It was thought that vibrations from nearby traffic had caused the problem but it was considered that occupiers and pedestrians were in no immediate danger. The properties were pulled down in 1971.

Above An unusual and dramatic picture, looking towards the centre of town, up through the *old* Woolshops. The photograph was taken in 1968 by Geoff Whippey. The scene is dominated by the large area of car parking on the right. On the left we can see the abattoir, its very bland facade giving no impression of the work which went on behind it. This area would be transformed by the new retail development which eventually covered about half the landscape in the view, but was once planned to be almost three times larger. The 'bottom end' of Halifax was once considered to be unappealing and to have little potential. Developments such as 'Eureka', the Calderdale Industrial Museum, the Sports Centre, the *latest* Sainsbury's store and the general tidying-up of the remaining older property around them has enhanced this location dramatically.

> **"THE BOTTOM END OF HALIFAX WAS CONSIDERED TO BE UNAPPEALING AND OF LITTLE POTENTIAL"**

Below: Cow Green, was once known as 'Halifax Green', but it takes its name from the fact that it was the area used as the town's cattle market. One street, now long since cleared and built upon, was called Swine Market, further evidence of the area's former use. In days gone by the area would have been busy with livestock and those who made their living rearing and trading them. This was the place frequented by farmers and dealers, and consequently there grew a steady demand for refreshments and alcohol, eagerly satisfied by one of the largest concentrations of public houses Halifax would ever see. These establishments were, on the whole, quite small as far as public houses go, but their numbers made up for any lack of floor space. Inns such as The Lord Nelson (closed in 1919), The Craven Heifer, which lasted until 1930, The King's Head, The Grand Junction which opened in 1897 and closed in 1968 and was formerly known as the Brown Cow, The Golden Plough, The Black Bull, The White Bear - the list goes on! Few people today would guess that the area was once so much more than just a busy thoroughfare at the top side of town, and fewer still would imagine that so many traditional pub names would adorn the street, only to be superseded by their modern equivalents 'The Pot O' Four' and ' Hangovers'. In the mid 1950s traffic lights were introduced at the junction of Cow Green and Pellon Lane. At the same time the paved area in front of Ebenezer Methodist Church was extended and a flower bed was incorporated.

During this period flower beds were very popular in Halifax which was gaining a reputation as the 'Flower Town of the North'.

Surprisingly, Cow Green was once the home of the Gibbet. It stood here and performed its grisly task before the permanent stone platform was constructed for it at the top of Gibbet Hill. Road widening changed the character of Cow Green in the mid 1960s, but perhaps the biggest development was the demolition of buildings made necessary by the erection of the multi-storey car park there in 1971.

The sub-way at Cow Green was completed in February 1970 at a cost of around £20,000.

Below: The greyness of this area around North Bridge is dramatically illustrated in this picture which dates from the late 1940s or early 1950s. The sign on the sturdy railway wall shows the location of the photographer's standpoint as Old Lane. To the right of that a sign left over from the recent hostilities points the way to a public air raid shelter. The greyness of the ironwork supporting North Bridge had been caused by years of smoke from the hundreds of chimneys in the area, including those leading lights in the pollution stakes just down the way at the power station. The hard working engines on the sidings below would obviously add to the grimy deposits and reinforce the reputation of this part of town as the 'Devil's Cauldron'. We should not leave this photograph without a mention of the *Pineapple Hotel* which was located at 127 New Bank and is seen on the right of the picture. The original Pineapple had been constructed here as long ago as 1772, but the one seen in the photograph dated from 1903. It lasted until 1968 when, like many other properties here, it fell prey to the demolition men.

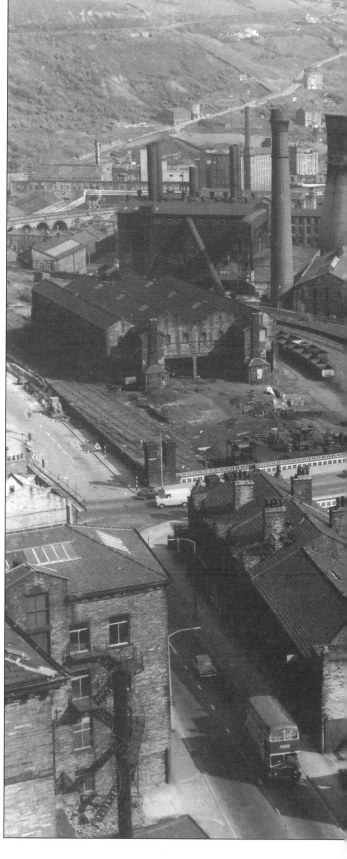

Above: "Smoke from the electricity power station fills the air of Halifax with pollution. There is no place in this county that requires more serious effort to implement this Clean Air Act than Halifax" So said a visiting councillor from Leeds when asked to comment on the efforts being made in the town to comply with the newly imposed regulations designed to combat air pollution.

The first smokeless zone was introduced in Halifax in October 1959 in accordance with the 1956 Clean Air Act.

It covered the very centre of the town, the boundaries being Union Street, Market Street, Northgate, Broad Street, New Broad Street, Cow Green, Lister Lane, the westerly boundary of the New Brunswick Street development area, Hopwood Lane, Bull Green, Barum Top, Fountain Street and Horton Street. September 1961 would see the introduction of smokeless zones at Mixenden and in the Skircoat area.

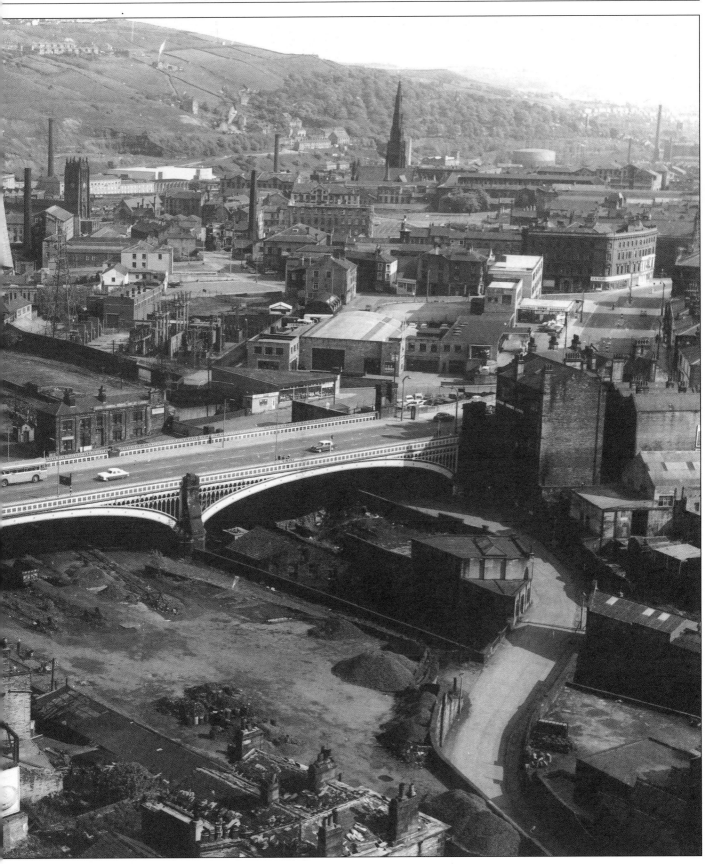

Above: An elevated view of an area which could once be described as the powerhouse of Halifax, with the gas and electricity works on the left, and their essential rail supply links and goods yards clearly shown in the foreground. The cooling towers which would later cause their weight in embarrassment and were often blamed for the fine, rain-like mist which would sometimes drift across town stand like a couple of discarded milk-churns in the picture. The local Vauxhall dealership with its modern low building can be seen beyond the end of North bridge, just across the way from *Cable Motors* the well-known supplier of motorbikes and three wheeled Reliant cars. The elegant North Bridge is seen in a way that is no longer possible since the building of the huge concrete flyover which now overshadows it. When it was opened North Bridge was not only one of the most elegant structures of its type, it held the record for having the lowest cost per square foot of the road across it, of any major bridge in the country.

Above and right: Two photographs that capture opposite viewpoints of New Bank. Looking at the this area now it is hard to believe that it was once one of the more densely populated locations within the borough of Halifax. The redevelopment of the town centre in the 1960s and 70s left the land around here rather bare and desolate. There had been plans and proposals to build much-needed housing here, but they were abandoned when it became clear that previously uncharted underground mining works and springs would have made the work too costly. In the dirty days before smoke control was introduced to

Halifax the residents of New Bank lived on the very rim of what was called the 'Devil's Caldron' - a graphic description of the pollution rising from the industrial area close to the town centre.

St. Joseph's Roman Catholic School is a well-known landmark in this area. It was built as the Portland Road Board School and opened in February 1878. It was bought by the Roman Catholic community in 1929, replacing the St. Joseph's school which had opened on the Southowram side of Godley Bridge in 1873.

The names of several public houses from the area will doubtless bring back memories: The Brickmakers Arms, Ramsden's The Wellington and The Great Northern Hotel, lower at North Bridge, were well supported in their day.

Four decades of good old fashioned service

RP Dowsland was established in 1955 by, not surprisingly, Mr RP Dowsland. He had previously worked in the field of electrical engineering when he worked for MF Farrar of Crossley Street.

Above: One of the company's earliest vehicles, a Ford Thames van with Mr Dowsland at its side.
Left: Mr Dowsland inside the shop in the 1960s.
Below: A 1960s view of the shop on Wesley Court with the old chapel to the right.

Following the retirement of Mr. Farrar, Mr Dowsland started his own business at Wesley Court which, being directly opposite the Town Hall steps is a premier position. The company have employed electricians and apprentices through the years. Mrs Dowsland managed the shop and carried out the office work.

Mike Hartley joined the company in 1976 as an electrician and continued to work there until February 1988. Mr Dowsland then retired, handing the firm over to Mike Hartley. Mrs Dowsland continued to work, showing Mrs Hartley her job.

The business still offers the same values as it always has, quality, customer care and expertise. It is these qualities that have made Dowsland's a well respected member of the local community and these which will see it through the next fifty years.

The field of electrics has changed immensely over the decades, although traditional values never do. Dowsland's still endeavour to provide their customers with courtesy and care.

Rice Jones & Smith - at the hub of the town's legal matters

To the uninitiated, the duties of a solicitor may seem routine and boring. This is not so. Each case has its own interest and its own problems. Mr. Robert Mackenzie tells of a Halifax client who retired to Bournemouth and died, leaving an estate of £1.2 million to be disposed of. It was left to the children of the client's cousin and the deceased's only instruction was, 'You'll find them when the time comes.' Mr. Mackenzie saw a lot of hard work ahead and the firm of Rice-Jones and Smith appealed to the Halifax Courier for help. As a result of the article that was published, however, Mr Mackenzie received a phone call from one of his client's old schoolfellows who had known all the people concerned. The legatees were all traced in a single afternoon!

Difficult times

Robert Mackenzie's father was not so lucky. Wallace Mackenzie had a client who died a bachelor and had not made a will. His grandparents had been displaced

persons in the First World War; his mother had been one of nine children.

Tracing the legatees was very complicated. Eventually all 70 of them were rounded up. When the residue of the estate had been divided by that number, there was not a great deal for each of them to be thankful for. The moral of this story is - make a will!

The beginnings of change

This firm of Halifax solicitors is an amalgamation, dating from the early 1970s, of two others. Rice, Jones & Smith, the first, was established towards the end of the last century. Mr. Smith and Mr. Rice-Jones were joined by Mr Smith's son who succeeded to the practice in the

1920s. Mr J.E. Smith, the son, ran the business himself until 1962 when he took into partnership Mr. John Adshead.

Mr. Smith's business had been mainly commercial and he was involved in the flotation of many well known companies. He retired from the Halifax practice in 1967. Mr. Adshead was then joined by Mr. Grayham Smith.

Wallace Mackenzie & Son

The other half of the amalgamation, had begun its existence in the 1890s as a one man firm run by Sam Hoyle. When he retired, the practice was taken over by Herbert Boocock and the office run by John Mackenzie, a managing clerk, who was then joined by his son, Wallace when he qualified in 1929. When Herbert Boocock died in 1947, Wallace Mackenzie took over, practicing in his own name. His son, Robert joined the business when he qualified in 1964. The firm then became Wallace Mackenzie and Son.

There have been a number of recent changes within the partnership and, with effect from 1st May 1997, the on-going partners are Robert Mackenzie, Michael Taylor, David Hofton and Steven Bonfield. Mr. Adshead continues to work as a consultant. The work of the practice now is primarily concerned with civil litigation, personal injury, matrimonial, child care and family work, conveyancing, employment law, litigation, company work and probate, wills and tax planning.

It has recently been decided to concentrate the firm's activities within the Halifax offices. Sub-offices in Brighouse and Sowerby Bridge have now closed. In addition to the partners and consultant already mentioned, the firm has a number of other highly qualified and specialised solicitors and legal executives. Together with trainees, they make a staff of over twenty-five. As the firm approaches the millennium, it looks forward to a future that will be as successful as its past - with high standards of customer service the key to achieving this aim.

Above: The modern legal practice which has a sympathetic approach to its clients. Left: A 1960s roof-top view of Commercial Street which shows Pearl House being built. This is now one of the firm's offices.

Excellence in property -with firm foundations

The life of an estate agent is not always routine. When Brearley-Greens were instructed by the relative of a certain, late Miss Holroyd to sell her house and auction the contents, they began their usual 'sorting out' exercise and found, in the attic and garden cellar room a water colour by Girtin and several others by David Cox Snr. Though the pictures were dirty and covered in dust, their colours were well preserved since they had been stacked in the dark. Sotheby's were approached and their Mr. James Miller authenticated the find. The Girtin alone was valued at between twenty and thirty thousand pounds.

More often, however, Brearley-Greens employees spend their time merely giving satisfaction to their customers, buyers and vendors of property in the Halifax area.

The firm was established in 1976 by Mr. Peter Green, a Fellow of the Society of Valuers and Auctioneers. Previously, he had been a partner in another auctioneering business. He set up to begin with at number seven Clare Road. His son, Richard, is the partner who heads the Residential Sales Division and Peter's wife, Carol, also

Above: This building was once the Borough Club and was sold by Brearley-Greens, going on to become the home of Flashmans public house. *Below:* The Hollins, Warley. Described in the brochure which accompanied its sale as 'a secluded mansion standing in its own grounds and woodlands on the edge of the beautiful Calder Valley', the picture shows the quality of the houses sold by Brearley-Green.

Left: A scene during an auction sale of antique silver in 1956. Peter Green, who went on to found Brearley-Greens can be seen second from the right. He was the sales clerk. Peter Green has been involved with the sales/auction business all his adult life. **Bottom left:** A house on 'The Rocks' which was sold by Brearley Green in the late 1970s. The site has now been redeveloped, this house being demolished and replaced by luxury flats. **Below and bottom right:** The present premises on Horton Street. This has been the company's home since 1985.

works for the company. In 1985, after nine years in Clare Road, a move was decided on.

The premises at twelve Horton Street, Halifax were purchased, gutted and refurbished. Business prospered there, despite the challenge of Banks, Insurance Companies and Building Societies entering the property market. Brearley-Greens' transactions in residential property are mainly in Calderdale and Kirklees. Brearley-Greens are also now one of the leading quality residential Estate Agents in Kirklees via their imposing town centre office in Huddersfield led by their Kirklees Partner, Mr. Chris Jowett. They deal in the complete range of domestic property, from the right house for a first time buyer to a mansion for the successful executive. The most expensive house to pass through the firm's hands sold for £600,000. In transactions involving land, of course, far higher sums change hands. The Commercial and Industrial Division deals nationwide under the leadership of the Commercial Division's Partner, Mr. Keith Cannon.

Brearley-Greens are proud to be traditional, in the sense that its senior staff are qualified not only to buy and sell property on behalf of their clients but also to guide them through all the legal processes that these exchanges involve. Standards of quality which are carried down through the years hold high importance, yet the company remains one of the most forward looking and successful companies in its field in the area, with the most modern equipment and approach to business. They are proud too of their unmatched local knowledge and their total independence in business matters. They plan to expand the "quality residential" and commercial divisions of the practice and to maintain their well established position.

Finn Gledhill - centuries of service

Finn Gledhill is one of West Yorkshire's major legal practices, providing a wide range of services to local, regional and national clients. It was formed by the amalgamation of three old Halifax general practices and took the firm from quill pens and ink to the latest Information Technology.

Godfrey, Rhodes and Evans dates from the 1850s and traded from premises above the York County Savings Bank. F.N. Dickie was the last survivor of an even older firm, Frederick Walker Son and Dickie, established in the 1700s. When he died, in 1965, Finn Gledhill, then known as Finn Gledhill & Co. bought No. 2 Harrison Road, part of their present premises.

In 1969 Horsley, Bairstow & Helliwell, first established in the 1880s, amalgamated with Finn Gledhill & Co.

The practice has grown rapidly. In 1962 it consisted of Hugh Finn and Michael Gledhill, together with one clerk and two secretaries. Presently, the practice has eight partners and forty staff and occupies premises on both sides of Harrison Road.

By the late 1960s No. 2 Harrison Road became too small to house the rapidly expanding firm, so a plan was considered to build a new four storey extension at the rear of No. 2. In view of the estimated cost, the practice decided instead to purchase No 1 Harrison Road from Pickles the Architect. No. 3 Harrison Road was added, with the Horsley Bairstow & Helliwell amalgamation. No. 4 was acquired when the Accountants, Whitham Smith Mitchell ceased to practice in the early 1980s.

Together these four properties form the firm's present headquarters. The firm is known locally as a progressive and sound general practice. It has a considerable

1700s
Robert Parker (1761 - 1796)
Robert Parker (1753 - 1761)
John Baldwin (1753 - 1761)
James Wrigglesworth 1796
Wrigglesworth & Thompson 1797
Wrigglesworth, Thompson & Stansfield 1815
Wrigglesworth & Parker 1824
Parker & Adam 1826
Adam & Emmett 1856
Emmet, Emmet & Kenny 1869
Emmet & Emmet 1871
Emmet & Walker 1876
F Walker & Son 1899
Frederick Walker, Son & Dickie 1945 - 1965

1870s
Godfrey Rhodes
Godfrey Rhodes & Evans
Richard Evans 1883
Lewis Rhodes 1904
Robert Kenworthy 1908
HW Roberts 1929
HWW Finn 1953
MW Gledhill 1962

1880s
J Pickles
Pickles Horsley & Co
Pickles Horsley Bairstow
Horsley Bairstow
Horsley Bairstow & Helliwell 1969

1965
Finn Gledhill & Co
Peter Hamlett 1967
William D Thomas 1967 (ret 1989)
John Helliwell 1969 (ret 1993)
David JL Lee 1969
John B Patchett 1969 (ret 1993)
Malcolm Nowell 1982
Carol Stevenson 1986
Elizabeth A Jones 1986 (ret 1990)
Stephen J Mattock 1989
Marc Gledhill 1990
Amanda Redfearn 1996

Name changed to Finn Gledhill in 1996

reputation for its national work, where the emphasis is on commercial property matters, especially all types of brewery work and estate and town and city centre developments. The commercial department also handles a large number of leases and financial work for all types of transactions and business ventures.

Private residential property sales and purchases represent a significant amount of the firm's practice and a new addition to the services offered is that of independent financial advice by a fully qualified I.F.A.

The firm has a substantial Probate and Trust Practice and is well known for the work it undertakes on behalf of charities. A particular strength is the handling of matrimonial disputes, licencing applications and appeals, criminal cases and civil claims. The practice has a computerised debt collection service and also deals with insolvency matters. More recently, it has specialised in Building Society repossessions.

The firm has high aims. In its practice purpose statement, it sets out to become and remain the outstanding law firm in Calderdale, whilst having considerable influence outside the locality and to provide the widest range of services to clients and so offer a genuine alternative to the large city practices. The firm is fully committed to being wholly professional, but seeks to retain its cheerful, friendly and approachable image with a fully dedicated staff.

Above: Finn Gledhill's Number 2, Harrison Road offices as they are today.
Top left: The origins of the three firms that amalgamated to form Finn Gledhill can be traced back to the 1700s. This line drawing of the North Bridge end of town, including the original stone bridge, shows the Halifax that existed at that time.
Left: The Finn Gledhill 'firm tree'.

Fred Moore: the Halifax TV and Radio pioneer

The story behind Halifax's best known domestic electrical goods retailer goes back three generations to just after the turn of the century. Fred Moore began trading in fancy goods and picture frames from his shop on Market Street. The early 1920s saw the birth of the wireless industry; people throughout Britain would construct primitive crystal sets at home in order to receive broadcasts from the handful of radio stations which were emerging just after the First World War.

Fred Moore was quick to see the potential that this offered and began selling the components such as valves and earphones to radio enthusiasts in the area. For a time these radio components were sold alongside picture frames and fancy goods in the Market Street shop but then, in the late 1920s manufactured sets became available and demand for them grew rapidly.

The original premises on Market Street.

Fred Moore quickly established an excellent reputation with all the leading manufacturers - all eager to appoint committed dealers who were familiar with the new technology and capable of offering the crucial after-sales service that the customers expected.

Sadly, Fred Moore died in 1954 and was succeeded by his son, Stanley Moore who had worked with his father in the business since 1926. A milestone in the development of the company came in the 1930s with the move to Southgate. This was long before the area was pedestrianised.

In the early 1950s the premises next door became available and Stanley Moore grasped the opportunity to expand the space in which to display the growing range of electrical goods. This coincided with the introduction of television in the Halifax area and these became a popular addition to the products sold in the store. At around the same time, a service department was opened out of town, o Skircoat Moor Road. Over the years the company had built up a large number of rental customers - with TVs, radios and other household electrical appliances on offer. These customers were supported by a team of repair and service personnel based at Skircoat Moor Road.

The third generation of the Moore family to join the business, Mr Howard Moore, began working for the firm in 1965. This was an exciting time for everyone concerned with the TV business, as the growth in household television ownership in the area took hold.

Howard moore, the current chairman and managing director recalls some of the more significant milestones; 'The advent of colour TV from 1969 onwards was perhaps the most exciting time for us. Sets were expensive, understandable so really because they were so much more sophisticated than black and white models....but that didn't put us off. Everyone wanted to be the first house in the street to have a colour set. Video recorders were the next major event in the home entertainment world and our branches were kept busy with the demand."

Recent changes in the retail environment in Halifax have affected Fred Moore Ltd. "It's not something I like to dwell on very much now," says Howard "but it is a great disappointment to me to see how many of the long established, independent businesses in the heart of the town centre have been forced to relocate because of increasing rents. Still, every cloud has a silver lining and the move to the present spacious showrooms on New Road has proved very popular with our customers."

Familiar to most Halifax folk, the shop on the Precinct was rented by Fred Moore from the 1930s until June 1995.

The present spacious premises on New Road.

At your leisure

an extension along Harrison Road) Jubilee, and Victory Works, (West Parade) and Empire Works, Huddersfield. Gledhill's expertise was put to good use during the war years, with the manufacture of many precision mechanisms for bombs and work on special military instruments for the war effort.

Top: The Railway Age came to Halifax in the 1840s. At one time the town had three railway stations serving it, the first being built at Shaw Syke in 1844. This was followed by a temporary structure constructed on the site of the present Horton Street station which dates from 1886. The station was known as 'Halifax Old' from 1890, 'Halifax Town' from 1951, and 'Halifax' from 1961. The two other railway stations serving Halifax were St.Paul's, which closed in 1917, and North Bridge which closed in 1955.

Above: The annual works outing was a treat that every member of staff would look forward to. Here we see employees from G H Gledhill & Sons Ltd. of Trinity Works at a seaside resort on the east coast. The story of their company starts in 1886 with the invention of an 'automatic cash till' with a mechanism for recording transactions on a roll of paper, in much the same way as modern tills perform today. The invention came at a good time, for the growth in retailing was about to gather momentum and demand for an accurate way of recording a large number of small transactions was enormous. The firm's first premises were at Broad Street, but later additions took place with property at Trinity Works (with

With the age of rail travel the implications for leisure were greatly enhanced for ordinary folk. Small communities on the coast, such as Blackpool, would soon become thriving holiday resorts, accessible to many for the first time as a result of the railways. Most Halifax people will have fond memories of organised trips, either through work or, just as likely, their church or Sunday School, to one of the coastal resorts. Here we see a party of trippers about to set off on theirs, obviously excited about the prospect!

Facing page: A tranquil scene showing the boating lake at Shibden Park in 1933. Perhaps the most surprising aspect of the scene is found in the top left corner of the picture. Careful scrutiny of the light-coloured rectangular shapes above the two blocks of houses, running alongside the road, reveals that these are large advertising hoardings. Few people using the road today would guess that the road leading to one of the town's most respectable suburbs was once lined with these large advertising signs. The photograph is very nicely framed and it is thought that the young people in the picture were art students on a field trip. It is known that the boating lake was much deeper than it is today when the picture was taken - up to 20ft deep in places by all accounts.

Below: Tea retailing was big business when the Sowerby Bridge Industrial Society constructed this finely detailed float on the back of a Bedford truck for a local gala procession. Many fortunes were made by companies which became involved in growing tea on the massive plantations in India, as well as retailing the beverage back in Britain. The picture dates from the mid 1950s - we can be fairly sure of that as the poster in the background refers to the Sowerby Bridge U.D.C elections in May 1954.

Below: The Odeon stands on the left of this picture, looking on as the much older buildings in the scene contemplate their fate. The building on the right, at the corner of Waterhouse Street, is the Wesley Chapel, built in 1829.

Right: A musical procession accompanied the 1952 Gala day in Sowerby Bridge. Members of a local brass band are seen here marching along Wharf Street. The offices of the Halifax Building Society can be seen in the top left of the picture. Wharf Street has always been the retail hub of Sowerby Bridge.

Above: The Mayor and Mayoress can just be made out on the extreme right of this picture as members of the Scout Band march past on their St. George's Day Parade in 1950. The distinctive 'Halifax' bus in the background adds to the atmosphere created in the scene, as does the Ovaltine poster on the gable end of the property lower down the street.

Left: There must have been tens of thousands of photographs taken by local people over the years of processions for the Charity Gala. This one, dating from 1969, is around 30 years old at the time of writing, so the young men of in the Boy's Brigade Band will now be in their late forties! Timothy Whites, the very popular chemists on the corner of this busy main street location, later merged with Boots the chemists. The year 1969 was the 13th Charity Gala in Halifax. There were 80 vehicles in the parade which began at Woolshops and ended at Manor Heath. The Maurice Jagger trophy for the best decorated charity float went to the Halifax Deaf Association. The 1969 Gala Queen was 20 year old Judy Richardson of Lightcliffe. After going through difficulties because of lack of financial support in the late 1980s, the annual charity gala continues to this day and will, doubtless, always be a part of summertime fun in Halifax.

> ## "1969 SAW THE 13TH ANNUAL CHARITY GALA IN HALIFAX"

Above: A charming photograph from the 1950s, featuring junior members of Sowerby Bridge St. John's Ambulance Brigade. The picture was taken just behind the Police Station, off Station Road; railway coal trucks are just visible on the right of the picture, above the lorry's cab. It is difficult not to be moved by the innocent, smiling faces of the youngsters as they proudly display their placards from the precarious platform on the *Calder Carbonising* lorry. It is likely that they would have been making their way up to Crow Wood Park as part of the Sowerby Bridge Gala procession.

> **"THERE WERE OVER TWENTY WELL-SUPPORTED CINEMAS IN THE DISTRICT"**

Above left: Mayor Sharp and members of Halifax R.U.F.C discuss tactics before a special dinner held in the team's honour. Note the trophy in front of the Mayor, no doubt the dinner was in aid of the team's recent success on the field. The picture dates from 1951.

Left: Another annual civic duty performed by the mayor, inspecting the Sea Cadets. The smartly turned-out youngsters, complete with rifles are seen outside the Gaumont Theatre at Ward's End. It is difficult to imagine today that people would condone the carrying of guns in a public place by young men like this. We have to remember though, that at the time this picture was taken the war had been over for only five or six years, and most people would have been totally 'signed -on' to the concept of Britain having a strong defence. 'The Gaumont' was initially opened as the 'Picture House' in 1913. It had the distinction of being the first cinema in Halifax to introduce talking pictures, in 1929, though some historians suggest that the first *talkies* were actually shown at the Palladium at King Cross. The name change to *Gaumont* took place only three years before this picture was taken, in 1948. Seating 1272, the venue later became a bingo hall until it was converted into two cinemas (Astra 1 and Astra 2), *and* a bingo hall, in 1973. Operations ceased in 1982 but entertainment recommenced here in 1988 when it opened as the Coliseum nightclub.

The age of the cinema came to Halifax in 1910 with the opening of the Electric, but audiences had to wait until 1929 for the arrival of regular "talking" features.

At the height of the cinemas' popularity there were over 20 well-supported venues in the district for fans of the flicks to enjoy. These ranged from the mighty 2,000 seater Odeon, to the smaller, almost forgotten local picture houses such as the *Ideal Pictures* (Pellon) and the *Pioneer* at Wheatley Lane, Lee mount.

"AT THE TIME IT OPENED, NOTHING IN THE SOUTHGATE M&S COST MORE THAN FIVE SHILLINGS"

Below: A group of delightful ladies with one or two male colleagues, all employees of Marks and Spencers Halifax branch, about to set off on a coach trip. The building behind the group on the right of the picture is the Rose and Crown public house. It is said that Daniel Defoe wrote part of his most famous work, *Robinson Crusoe,* here on a visit to Halifax. The historic pub was acquired by the company and demolished in 1958 to make way for an extension to the store. Marks and Spencer's have been trading in Halifax since 1933 and the premises have been extended greatly over the years. Remarkably, the opening of the Halifax branch coincided with rapid expansion of Britain's favourite retailer, 27 other new stores were opened in the same years! At the time it opened nothing in the Southgate branch of Marks and Spencer cost more than five shillings.

Above: Staff at a Marks and Spencer staff dinner, thought to originate from about 1960. The gentleman seated third from the right, on the opposite side of the table, is Councillor Albert Berry of Boothtown. Councillor Berry was kind enough to supply many of the photographs contained within this book; he worked at the store for many years after spending much of his working life with British Railways at Halifax railway station.

Above: The Palace Theatre stood at Ward's End, opposite the rebuilt Theatre Royal which was situated here from 1905. Many readers may remember that the *Palace* was known affectionately by local people as 'the sweetest theatre in the land'. This was came about because the builders who constructed it faced difficulties when frosty weather affected the way their cement had been drying. Their solution was to mix sugar with the mortar, hence the origin of the nick-name. *The Palace* was hailed as 'a very fine and substantial establishment' when the curtain went up on the first performance in August 1903.

The theatre served Halifax until 1959 when, with the advent of *television and bingo,* it was pulled down and replaced by a shop and office development. This development included premises which went on to be the area's tax offices, with a popular Wimpy bar located on the corner, beneath them. A busy fried fish restaurant and takeaway is situated here at the time of writing.

Caldene Clothing Company: riding wear with a long pedigree

The history of Caldene Clothing Company goes back to 1922 when George Uttley started the enterprise with his brothers in law, Jack and Walter Lord. He was born in Hebden Bridge in 1898 and after attending the local school started work in the clothing trade when he was 13.

The young George was called up for army service in 1917 and subsequently joined the London Rifles, went to the front in France and was wounded. After demobilisation in 1919 he returned to the clothing industry in Hebden Bridge.

measurement form, which they returned giving choice of cloth, full set of measurements and appropriate money. Apparently, postage was cheaper if book and cloth were sent in separate envelopes. Customers were asked to return the styles and samples, whether or not they ordered. A reply-paid sticky label was enclosed for this. The cloths in the swatches were made according to Caldene's specifications and they contracted for weaving and dyeing so that every process was under their direction.

Even though times were different between the wars and business, compared with the 90s, both formal and leisurely, Caldene's workers and customers, as revealed in old catalogues seem to have been on extremely good terms with each other.

Children's garments were available with "generous inlays" on seams so "the garment can be made to grow with its young wearer". This was not a throw-away society. Customers were assured, "We shall always be happy to quote a lower price for the making of children's garments"!

Caldene offered a painstaking service. "Take special notice of the fact that Caldene breeches are not cut from patterns. Every pair is specially drafted by a draughtsman master-cutter from the measurements you send in. In this way you get a perfect fit....Our cutter can form a mental picture of your figure" (Horrors!)

Above: The Mytholmroyd works have been extended no less than seven times since this 1930s drawing. *Below right:* Mr George Uttley, the company's founder.

The business was founded with just £15 from each of the three partners and set up in a former army hut. The mills around Hebden Bridge had a long reputation for weaving hard wearing cloths, such as corduroy and cavalry twill, and these fabrics were used by an expanding local clothing industry which produced long-lasting clothing for working men.

From the beginning, George Uttley concentrated on making riding breeches for farmers and agricultural workers. Worn with leggings or long stockings, the breeches were "clean on the legs" and all made to measure - by mail order!

Sounds unlikely? Actually, customers wrote in to ask for cloth patterns, style booklets and a self-

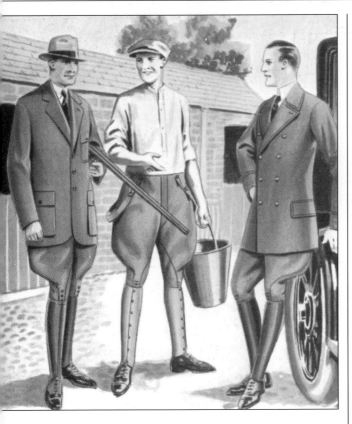

*Above: Smart travelling clothes and working gear were both made with meticulous care. **Below right:** Pages from the mail order catalogue sent out to customers between the two world wars.*

When Caldene received an order a cutter cut out the garment after the individual measurements had been drafted on to the material. After cutting, garments were transferred to the machine room where tailoresses made up the garments.

Radio was installed to entertain the women as they worked. Another team dealt with buttonholing, buttoning and serging. Buckskin strapping was hand-stitched on. "We should like to stress," the catalogue explained, "the importance of having mock-buckskin strappings fitted between the legs to grip the saddle and prevent wear taking place." Next, "finishers" completed the garment. Better quality ones had considerable quantities of hand stitching. Finally. steam pressers removed creases and flattened seams.

"Occasionally," customers were assured, "we are asked to fulfil an order very quickly indeed... and in such exceptional circumstances we will do so with pleasure; at the same time, we rely upon customers not to ask us unless the need is very pressing."!

The customers were appreciative. "The man whose name I am enclosing remarked upon the cut of same. (breeches) Please send him patterns and you will have another regular customer.' Another wrote in, "I was just a bit frightened lest I couldn't use the tape properly, but evidently your chart can be relied upon to do its work."- Well, well! The customer blaming himself for what might go wrong. Times have changed.

In the early days the business was very much a family affair, with wives and daughters helping with the sewing, but the work force had increased with the orders. In 1936 a small factory was built just down the road in Mytholmroyd which proved to be the nucleus of the business today. Mr. G. T. Uttley's only son, Kenneth, joined the business in 1936 straight from school and continued in the firm until he volunteered for the RAF in 1941. During the war, production was largely turned over to motor cyclists' pantaloons for army dispatch riders and breeches for the ladies of the land army. Here too Caldene found favour. One customer wrote, "I don't know when the breeches will wear out. I can account for 8,000 miles' motor cycling in them, yet they are as good as new.' *contd. overleaf*

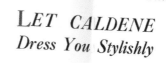

LET CALDENE
Dress You Stylishly

Good cut and good material are the two outstanding merits of Caldene Ladies' Tailoring.

How the Cut is achieved.

Take special notice of the fact that Caldene breeches are not cut from patterns. Every pair is specially drafted by a draughtsman master cutter from the measures you send in. In this way you get perfect fit and the best possible style for your figure. Our cutter can form a mental picture of your figure from the measurements you supply and thus can fit you superbly. Also you choose the cut you want from the styles shown in the catalogue so you have plenty of choice.

Measurements—We guarantee to fit perfectly. Our simple self-measure chart (which CALDENE originated) will make it perfectly simple.

This Guarantee Protects you Fully.

Note every one of the following points :

(1) Every garment is made in our own workrooms—by tailors and genuine Yorkshire breeches cutters who have all the tradition attached to Yorkshire cut and the leading London cutting Diplomas and experience as well.

(2) The cloths are made to our specifications, and we contract for weaving and dyeing so that every stage of manufacture is under our direction. Also great economies are effected—and this is one of the reasons for our remarkably keen prices. Turnover and big production make us unbeatable. The cloths are made in our own district. No transport charges to add to costs.

(3) Six Months' fair wear and tear guarantee. We guarantee every pair against defects in material and workmanship, subject only to fair wear and tear. We are the only firm that dare offer this guarantee. See catalogue (back page of cover) for further details.

CALDENE CLOTHING COMPANY
Hebden Bridge, Yorks.
Phone 157

After the end of the war, the market altered and the business changed from being solely a mail order company into making ready-to-wear breeches and jodhpurs for distribution to shops and stores. In the early 1960s, the 'Cotswold' and 'Pacemaker' one-way stretch jodhpurs were introduced, made from what had been designed originally as a ski cloth with warp stretch.

In 1967 the 3rd generation of the family, Mr. Carl Uttley, joined the business after qualifying as a production engineer at Leeds College of Clothing Technology. The 1970s saw the introduction of two-way stretch jodhpurs from nylon/lycra knitted fabrics which remain the same today.

The 'Cavalier' range of thermal garments were pioneered and developed in 1979 from a cloth with a

cotton backing. Jackets and hunt coats were added to the Caldene range in the 1970s. Over the decades, there have been many 'specials' produced, including gamekeeper suits, mounted police breeches, chauffeurs

suits, breeches for comedy films and even sets of racing leathers for riders in the Isle of Man TT races.

The first export order was made for a tack shop in Canada and, since then, Caldene Riding wear has been sent to most parts of the world where riding is popular. A comparatively new product, recently developed, is a ladies' riding habit officially approved for members of the Side Saddle Association.

On 20th November 1991, the company was honoured by a visit from the Princess Royal in her capacity as patron of the British Knitting and Clothing Export Council. She was given a warm reception from the workers on that cold November day and was then escorted by Mr. Carl Uttley to every department where she impressed the work force with her knowledge of and interest in equestrian clothing. She was presented with £3,000 for the charity she and the company have long supported, Riding for the Disabled.

Caldene presented HRH with riding clothes for her children, Peter and Zara. She visited the company's day nursery, opened on November 2nd 1991, the company's investment in skilled female employees.

Over the years the Uttley family has resisted takeover and merger offers and resolutely remained a private company that emphasises individual attention. Today, after seven extensions to the original factory buildings and with two generations still active in the business, Caldene is one of the most modern factories in Britain, with a new computer system that can cope with in excess of 10,000 items. They are amongst the most progressive riding wear manufacturers in the UK, an enviable inheritance for Carl's son, Adam.

Above: More hard work in the machine room in this 1950s view. Facing page, small picture: Mr George Uttley and his son Kenneth, personally checking work in the Inspection Room during the 1940s. Left: HRH, the Princess Royal chats to Carl Uttley and his sister, Jill Butters during her 1991 visit. Right: This model is wearing an outfit which displays some of the riding wear that Caldene manufacture and sell.

From small acorns to large oaks....

Andy Thornton Architectural Antiques Limited is a company which began life quite by chance. Andy Thornton, armed with a Bachelor of Education Degree in Creative Design and qualifications to teach woodwork, set off with his wife Kate, to work his way around the world. Whilst working as a joiner in Philadelphia, Andy found himself fitting out an architectural antiques showroom. This led on to repairing salvaged merchandise, which in turn led to an offer of work by a Californian customer (John Wilson) on the West Coast.

This was the start of a lucrative partnership which funded Andy and Kate's travels and established the basis for Andy's business. John Wilson would source antiques from all over the world and then employ Andy to organise huge annual auctions. In between these sales Andy and Kate continued their travels.

In 1975 they returned to England and purchased a derelict farmhouse in Rastrick, near Elland. The company was born. The main object of the business was salvaging period architectural antiques and shipping them to the USA for auction. Nostalgia for the traditional American bar and restaurant was in full swing; old pub fittings,

panelling, doors and windows were in great demand. When the genuine article became harder to find, Andy employed his first workers. Their job was to convert salvaged items into saleable products.

A new market was needed in 1980 because of a weak American Dollar and the recession. The breweries, impressed by what they had seen in the USA, were ready for a change - and so was Andy Thornton. The company soon established itself as a major supplier to the leisure industry in England and Europe. By this time Spike Bagshaw and Fred Standbrook were directors with the responsibility for designing and building pub and restaurant interiors. Andy used his American contacts to source new Tiffany shades and outdoor lighting. The reproduction side of the business began to grow with great speed and today, over 4,000 stock items are available.

The company is now divided into three divisions - Architectural Antiques, Catalogue Products and Design & Contracting. A strong and highly successful business, it employs 200 people, having a world wide reputation for design, innovation and quality.

Few companies can match this expertise. Skilled craftsmen in wood, glass and metal restore salvaged antiques and create new designs. Designers and project managers work with skilled architects to design stunning interiors for the leisure industry worldwide and knowledgeable buyers travel the world searching out architectural antiques and sourcing new products.

Nowadays half of the products are sold abroad, mirrored by the presentation of the Queens Award for Export to the company in 1994. Andy Thornton was also awarded an MBE for services to export two years later in 1996.

Left: We all had to start somewhere! Andy Thornton in 1975.
Top right: *This magnificent American bar was built in Andy Thornton's Elland workshops. Bartenders for the day are directors, Fred Standbrook and Spike Bagshaw.* ***Below:*** *From humble beginnings, the firm is now one of Calderdale's larger employers, with 200 staff.*

Hebden Cord - three generations of proud workmanship

A Hebden Bridge weaver, Edward Pickles, went off to serve his country in the First World War. In 1922, back home with his £40 demobilisation money, he set up the Hebden Cord Company - in his own attic. His venture producing made-to-measure riding breeches did well so that he was soon able to establish business premises in West End. Continuing to flourish, the business moved in 1946 to the present site at Old Gate.

Family ties

After the second world war, Edward made his son, Granville, a partner and in the early 1960s, Granville's daughter, Jan became an employee. At the age of 21, after proving her competence, she became a director. Tragedy followed (not attributable to Jan!) as fire gutted the building. Business had to transfer back to the Pickles' home until machinery and cloth could be replaced. The company

was at least fortunate in so far as the local business community proved very sympathetic and helpful.

Traditional values

The original cloths used by Edward are still popular, though none of it any longer costs eleven old shillings for a 56 inch width! The firm began trading by mail order and this aspect of the business still continues. Most garments are made of British cloths, woollens, tweeds, cavalry twills, corduroys and whipcords, etc., though an Austrian fabric is used for Norfolk jackets and plus-fours and stretch Helenca from Italy is used in some sports wear.

Demand in the UK is generally from estates for shooting suits, keepers' suits etc.. Garments are exported to the USA, Canada, Australia, Japan and throughout Europe. The Pickles family is proud to offer good workmanship, good quality fabrics and value for money.

Back in 1922 when Edward began his business in his attic, he could not even begin to imagine the speed in which it has grown over the decades, as well as the respect in which it held in the local community and beyond. At seventy five years old the company is truly established within its field and will continue to be so for many years to come.

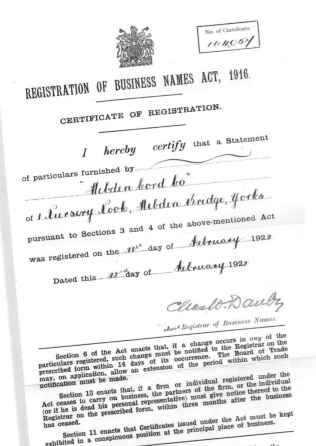

Above: The company's present site at Old Gate, Hebden Bridge. Left: The certificate of registration given to Edward Pickles when he founded his business.

At work

A fascinating picture of the Piece Hall, showing it in use as a wholesale fish, fruit and vegetable market, a function which began in 1871 and continued for more than a century. A mixture of horses, carts and early commercial vehicles is featured, and one or two familiar trading names can be made out on the various signs and motors in the picture. 'Jaggers' began trading as a fish retailer in 1881 and they are thought to be the longest established fish retailer in Halifax - and one of the oldest in the country. The high walls and ample enclosed area of the Piece Hall, located near to the heart of the town, proved ideal for the wholesale fresh food trade. Over the years the fabric of the building deteriorated and moves were made to have the Piece Hall renovated as more people began to appreciate the value of their town's historic buildings and monuments. The D.O.E designated the Piece Hall a Grade One building of architectural and historical interest. A renovation programme costing over £350,000 was undertaken and the Piece Hall was reopened in July 1973 to great public acclaim.

Below: An elevated view of the Piece Hall which will be unfamiliar to most younger readers. It shows the facility in use as a wholesale fruit, fish and vegetable market, with the cooling towers and power station in the middle distance. Just right of centre, on the horizon, the spire of St. Thomas's Church at Claremount can be seen. Much of the terraced property around St.Thomas's Church, was cleared in the mid 1960s as part of the town's slum clearance programme. Many people at the time considered St. Thomas's lucky to remain as it does, dominating the skyline above New Bank. At one time the church was down to 12 members, and most of them were people who had been re-housed in other districts after their own homes had been pulled down. There have been many changes at St. Thomas's - the most dramatic of which being after the spire was struck by lightning and subsequently pulled down in 1971. The building dates from 1857 when plans for it were first discussed. Several doubters questioned the proposed location of the church, suggesting that the high winds in this elevated location were strong enough to blow it over. Building work progressed rapidly and the first service was held there in 1860.

Right: A view of the inspection of the local police force, an annual event which involved the mayor of the day and the local Chief Constable. The scene dates from the beginning of the 1950s, most of the officers here would have served in the Second War which had ended only five or six years earlier.

Below, right: Annual police inspections were a matter of routine at one time, not just in Halifax, but for every force in the country. The police were organised in smaller units than is the case today, and towns like Halifax had their own Chief Constable. This photograph shows a parade of neatly turned out Officers with their motor vehicles lined up in order according to their registration numbers.

Office work in the early 1950s was very different to what people are used to today. These young ladies are seen toiling away at Hoffmans Garage, on Huddersfield Road. Note the size of the switchboard, entirely typical of the time, probably dealing with no more than three or four outside lines, but, by today's standards, large enough to house a system capable of serving a small village. It is easy to forget how labour intensive the administrative side of any business was, even thirty or forty years ago; computerisation has changed the world of work radically, and a drive to break down the barriers between job holders by making people 'multi-skilled' has had a vast impact on office workers on a world-wide scale.

Top: More than sixty members of the Sowerby Bridge St. John's Ambulance Brigade posed for this photograph on land next to the Rochdale canal. The date is not precisely known, but is thought to be sometime in the 1930s. Some clues to the picture's date of origin are the distinctive clothes worn by the non-uniformed ladies, and the medal worn by the man in his thirties to the left of the group. It is probable that he earned the medal in the Great War.

Above: A group of soldiers in the Halifax area. Little is known about the men featured here, the picture is typical of thousands held in the possession of householders the length and breadth of Halifax and is bound to rekindle memories of military matters and relatives, past and present, who served their town and their country. Halifax can be proud of her contribution in wartime. The town ranked among the best in terms of fund raising for fighter aircraft and battleships, not to mention the distinguished records of the brave men who fought at the front. Unlike some neighbouring towns Halifax did not experience widespread bomb damage. In all there were eleven recorded bombing incidents in the district, including the worst where eleven people lost their lives in the Hanson Lane area. Blackout regulations were strictly enforced so that no clue would be given away to the enemy bombers. A surprising statistic is the number of prosecutions which took place of people who had flouted the blackout; 1700 prosecutions in 1940, resulting in fines of up to £200 per week being collected by the authorities. Railings around parks and public buildings were cut down and recycled for the war effort, and large concrete shelters were built near schools and factories in case of enemy air raids.

Paper and packaging pioneers at Sheard

The business of Samuel Sheard was established at Woolshops, Halifax in 1860 as a distributor of paper bags and wrappings for the textile industry. The business continued for almost a century in the same vein, growing and prospering until in the 1940s it was relocated at the bottom of Horton Street, in Imperial Buildings, the building which now houses the Imperial Crown Hotel.

A family business

At this time, the company was being run by Charles Whittaker, who had taken over the reins from Samuel Sheard. Charles retained control until the 1960s when his sons, Brian and Eric Whittaker took charge.

expanded, purchasing Hollins Mill in Greetland.

Ten years later the company had grown to such an extent that it was able to buy out a small waste paper recycling company, Charles Heath & Son at Range Bank, Boothtown. This created an enormous impetus to expand. Both sides of the business were centralised at Hollins Mill, enabling the company to house all its operations under one roof, although both sides of the business kept their original names.

In 1986 Sheard Packaging, as it had become known, moved into its present premises at Calder Street, Greetland, to a site previously occupied by Lumby's Engineering.
The present Managing Director, John Whittaker joined the business in 1964, straight from school as a warehouseman, working his way up the ladder. When he married in 1970, his wife, Barbara, also joined the company and is today the company secretary.

Diversification

Due to the volatile cycle of prices in waste paper, it was decided that the company needed a different type of business to carry it through the slump periods in the waste paper trade and ten years ago the company began to produce corrugated cartons. This proved to be a wise move as now, this side of the business accounts for 60% of the business.

Phoenix from the ashes

A fire, which rampaged through Imperial Buildings during the 1950s meant that the business was forced to move again, across the road to India Buildings and in 1960 the company

Sheard Packaging has a continuous policy of investment in new plant and the modernisation of the premises. It is these aims, as well as the continued support from customer, suppliers and employees alike that will carry Sheard Packaging forward into the next millennium.

Left: A panoramic view of West Vale, looking towards Halifax, taken in the 1940s. Sheard Packaging moved to Greetland in 1960.
Above Left A picture of a Samuel Sheard & Son lorry, which would have been a familiar sight on the roads of Halifax in the early 1960s.
Top: Still in the early 60s. this time loading up in Rochdale Road, Greetland.

"Sorry I'm late but a woman kept me talking." The Nethercoats story

Eric Nethercoat was born in Sheerness, Kent. During the Second World War, as a soldier he was stationed in Halifax. It was here that he met his wife, Pauline and they chose to settle down in the area. The war was tough on Eric; he was captured twice and taken as a prisoner of war. The first time he escaped, he was recaptured but then, when he tried again, he got away by climbing up and over the roofs. He ran into the Italian countryside and was harboured by a local family who became his life long friends.

Eric's vow

Due to the fact that he developed frostbite in his toes during his spell as a Prisoner of War, on arrival back in England he was grounded. It is said that he remained thereafter extremely sensitive about people standing on his feet. With good reason! As he wasn't available for active service he went to work for the Ministry of Works. This stood him in good stead for the future and he vowed to earn enough to start up on his own one day.

This photograph was sent to Pauline by Eric in July 1947.

The North/South Divide

Eric knew that everyone has to start somewhere so after the war he got a job with Mr Crossley of Spring Edge as a jobbing joiner. Even then the North/South divide was in

evidence. Eric being a Southerner found it very difficult to make himself understood. Whilst doing a troughing job in King Cross one day, he asked the lady of the house for a 'pile'. She stared at him nonplussed for a while and asked

A picture dating from a similar period to the one on the left, showing Eric and Pauline enjoying a day trip in Sheerness, Eric's home town.

him, "A pile of what?" He repeated his question and this went on for quite some time until the penny dropped. "Oh, you mean a bucket!" she said as she went into the house to fetch one.

From the back of a handcart

Eric faced a blow when his employer unexpectedly committed suicide and Eric realised that this was probably as good a time as any to set up on his own. With Pauline helping from an office at home in Elmscote Avenue, he worked from the back of a handcart for a couple of years, with a small workshop at Hyde Park, doing odd jobs for local businesses and the general public. It was a wonder in the early days that anything ever got done. Eric had a terrible memory and had a habit of always being late for appointments and when he did finally arrive he would always say, "Sorry I'm late but a woman kept me talking." Over the years this became a catchphrase amongst friends and family.

Slow growth

He moved his business in 1952 to Dundas Street, employing two people. Pauline shared her time between working for the business and bringing up a family of one daughter and two sons. Eric then went into partnership and moved to Bell Hall, remaining there for four years. They were hard times for Eric and Pauline, the business barely made enough to support them and it was with some regret that Eric ended the partnership and moved on his own to Nichol Street, Spring Edge. Soon Eric was employing six people.

Eric and Pauline at a celebration in the early 1970s.

Taking a well earned break! David Harris (left) who became the Managing Director and is now semi-retired. David Midgley (centre) recently became contracts manager. They are seen in this 1960s picture with a customer.

David Harris joined the company at Nichol Street in 1959 and he was later to become the foreman.

Tragedy and decision

In 1966 the company faced its final move to Copley where it has remained ever since. Eric and Pauline's eldest son, Paul joined the company in 1970, straight from school, beginning as an apprentice. The premises allowed for expansion and expand the company did until hit with a blow in 1976 when sadly, Eric unexpectedly died of a heart attack. Pauline Nethercoat and David Harris had a serious decision to make; to stick with it or pack it in? They decided to stick with it and the firm was incorporated as a

limited company in 1977. David became Managing Director, Pauline became Chairperson and son, Paul became the Foreman.

Hope for the future

Happily over the next few years the company grew, and when David semi-retired in 1996 Paul took over as managing director with Pauline keeping a watchful and maternal eye on things, reinforcing the company's image as a family business, which has always been the underlying philosophy.

Nowadays, the company manufactures and fits quality specialised joinery for banks, building societies and major retail groups, i.e. Calvin Klein of New York. Now employing 28 local people, all skilled in their field, Nethercoats looks to the future with confidence. With two generations of the family already actively involved with the business, it is hoped that the third generation will carry the company's expertise forward into the next millennium.

The management of Nethercoats, from left: David Midgley, Paul Nethercoat, David Harris and Pauline Nethercoat, wife of the founder, is seated at the front.

The boy-scout who borrowed £100 to start a business

The origins of Nu-Swift are extremely unusual. They began as a chance meeting between a Danish Boy-Scout and a well-respected member of the Sheffield community on a warm mid-summer Bruges day in 1923.

Two years later, when Albert Harland was elected a Member of Parliament, he received a note of congratulations from that same Boy Scout, Find Graucob. At first, not recognising the name, he replied with thanks and then only later remembered the name.

The two men met for dinner at the House of Commons and Graucob outlined his idea for a new business. At that time he was working for a small London bank which was in imminent danger of closure. He therefore wanted to use the knowledge he had gained in previous employment with a Danish manufacturer of vending machines to supply automatic cigarette machines. The older man offered to lend him £100 to start out in this new venture, an offer that was gratefully received.

The following few years were an uphill struggle, but in time 'FG's' company became the largest of its type in England. So much so, in fact, that Graucob was then able to purchase a small company in West Yorkshire, diversifying his interests and laying the foundations for the successful company it is today.

The early days
Nu-Swift itself started life back in 1933 as a small engineering company manufacturing fire extinguishers in Elland. The company continued along in this vein , supplying local companies with their extinguishers until the Second World War, when it underwent a transformation.

The take-over and the beginnings of global recognition
Extinguisher production had been increased in response to demand from such bodies as the British Admiralty, who, at that time, were losing more ships through on-board fire than when engaged in enemy action.

In 1943 Nu-Swift came under Mr Graucob's management and its operation was reorganised and rationalised, becoming more sales and marketing orientated. The company ventured into the export market, establishing a presence in Scandinavia. Today, these export activities are on a global scale and account for 68% of manufacturing output.

Service and maintenance
In 1952 Nu-Swift launched a service and maintenance operation which still forms a vital part of its operation and the company grew steadily over the following decades until, by Mr Graucob's retirement in 1975, Nu-Swift had become a force to be reckoned with.

Generale Incendie
Under the guidance of the new chairman, Ivan Dorr, the company maintained a pattern of steady growth until, in 1984, it merged with Tony Murray's French fire extinguisher company, Generale Incendie. This move led to a further period of rapid growth and development.

"*The Happy Band*"
WHO ARE DETERMINED THAT BRITAIN SHALL NOT BURN

With Best Wishes for a Happy Christmas
from THE NUSWIFT ENGINEERING COMPANY LIMITED · ELLAND

Mr Murray has been the driving force behind an increasingly profitable company - from a turnover of £13 million and pre-tax profit of £600,000 in 1981 to a turnover almost trebled and a pre-tax profit of £6 million in 1986.

Dramatic growth

In that year Nu-Swift acquired Sicli, the largest manufacturer of fire extinguishers in France for a price tag of £5 million. Production was transferred to the French factory, the premises at Elland remaining as an administration and distribution base. By 1989, turnover and profits had risen dramatically to £440 million and £34 million respectively.

New developments

February 1990 saw further change for Nu-Swift, the company disposing of its French operations for £184 million. As a result, the decision was made to re-open its manufacturing facility in Elland. This unit is equipped with the latest fabrication and finishing equipment and was awarded the British Standard in recognition of its quality system. The recommencement of manufacturing has meant re-establishment with many well known local suppliers.

The production facility is the latest stage in the steady development of the company. Streamlining of the administration operation has seen the establishment of a fully trained customer service group, ready to give the company's customers all the help and advice they need.

While the core business is very much focused on fire extinguishers, Nu-Swift also supplies a range of portable fire protection and safety equipment, including fire blankets and fire signs. This has meant that a company with such a proud history can look forward to the future with confidence.

Above: A postcard dating from the 1930s, before the time when Christmas cards were the usual method of greeting.
Facing page, top: Find Graucob.
Facing page, bottom: Nu-Swift employees welcoming Mr and Mrs Find Graucob when the company was taken over in 1943.
Right: Mr Tony Murray, current Chairman of Nu-Swift.

A hi-tech firm based in Greetland that began in Germany almost 150 years ago

Freudenburg Nonwovens is the name of a Greetland based company that has its origins in another place at another time. In 1849 in southern Germany, Carl Johann Freudenberg purchased an old tannery in Weinheim, near Heidelberg. He set up a high quality leather business which prospered and achieved important trade links worldwide.

In the 1930s, when the leather industry declined, Freudenberg began producing crankshaft seals for engines, made at first of leather but later of rubber. Freudenberg still deals with the automotive industry and in 1956 they developed metal-to-rubber bonded components that control vibrations in engines and transmission units.

In 1948, however, their experiments in leather processing led to the development of a new type of material, 'nonwovens'. This was a very versatile, sheetlike structure with textile characteristics. Freudenberg are still the premier producers of nonwovens.

In Halifax

Meanwhile, on the Greetland site there was a mill popularly known as Belle Isle. Shortly after the turn of the century, workers would appear there in clogs, corduroys and red mufflers, smoking clay pipes. The office workers would stand at high

desks and only the typists were allowed to sit. The dye workers were given just a twenty minute break for their lunch and even the managers had to 'clock on' alongside the workers. There were no holidays with pay, the dyehouse was freezing and the work was heavy but in spite of this, according to the memories of Mr. Harry Parr, an employee for 50 years, the workers were usually in good spirits. Work was scarce sometimes but it was shared out equally so that no-one was sacked.

Mr. Parr remembers many 'characters' from those days. Jack Sharp, a manager, cooked his own dinner in his office every day. Walt Smith, a shop floor worker, was a knur and spell player and keen clay pigeon shooter. A fitter, Fred Barker, carried two steel rules, one for work and one to stir his tea! Once a week, 'Tripe Joe' Kitson would

bring a large basket to work to sell his tripe to the workers. At certain times during the day, the works buzzer sounded and local people set their clocks by it. The dye works had an efficient fire brigade that held weekly practices.

In 1923/4, Bradford Dyers' Association built two blocks of houses, known as Silverdale Terrace, for its own people to buy. After a £45 government subsidy the price to workers was £445, which they paid at a few shillings a week.

The canteen was three ex-army huts. For a charge of one penny, the canteen staff would cook whatever food the workers brought with them for lunch.
In 1925/6 a Silk department opened, but in 1929 the dyeing and finishing of woollen cloth stopped. Some of the woollen workers transferred to the silkworks but many were left out of work.

And how they got together......
Early in 1950 an Irishman, Bill Blackwood, set up an importing business. He operated from London, making arrangements with the Viledon department in Weinheim to market Freudenberg's products within the UK. He created the name Vilene and registered his company as Vilene Ltd. Blackwood's business ran into difficulties in 1954, partly

because of the cheap fibres available already in Britain and partly because of import tariffs. *contd overleaf*

*All the pictures on these pages date from the 1960s. **Above:** The delivery end of the batching machine. **Facing page:** Cross laying the carding fleece. **Centre:** Dating this picture would be very easy indeed, simply by looking at the fashions shown. This was Bondina's Vilene Studio, the workshop of clothing technicians who 'served industry and the public'. It was the 'testing ground' for applications and performance of existing products and new developments. **Below:** The open plan sales administration office. It is difficult to imagine that in those days computers were practically unheard of. No self-respecting office today would be without one, yet back then, the work still got done and all of it done manually!*

Left: At the time of this picture dating from 1969, this was the largest finished stock warehouse in the country and was capable of holding 3 million yards of Vilene. The sheer size can be discerned by the tiny figure of a woman (bottom centre).

The new company was named BONDINA. It had an initial staff of 15, continued their employment there until retirement. Premises were also leased in London, in St. James Street, where Bondina Sales Ltd. was formed. Meanwhile BDA was having further setbacks. Nylon had become the popular material for lingerie and as they could not process nylon, the company at Greetland closed and Freudenberg took over all the space. It was a very amicable arrangement. BDA's partners expressed appreciation of all past contacts with Freudenberg, and, on the latter's behalf, Professor Kraft said they had had "not only a partnership but a friendship."

contd. He decided it would be a good idea if the goods were manufactured in England. He was acquainted with a director of the Bradford Dyers' Association, Eric Padgett, and BDA had done Dyeing and finishing for Freudenberg in the past. BDA had space available and, eventually, Freudenberg's chose their site to begin operations in this country. In 1956 the first lot of machinery was shipped over and installed in the 80,000 square feet of space. Work was under way by May 1956 and the first sales made in September.

Above: A section of the laboratory where all Bondina products were subjected to the most exacting tests to guarantee the reliability of standards.

Left: The blended fibre, ready for the next stage in the production process - 'carding'.

Bondina takes over

BDA had steadily declined and by 1962 all its operations moved from the Greetland location. So, within six years, Bondina had taken over the whole site. As the demand for nonwovens increased, several extensions were added to the original buildings. 1968 saw the first of these, the 2nd in

1974, whilst the two phases of the fourth building came in 1988/9. By then the total floor space was 50,000 square feet and Bondina was one of the foremost producers of nonwovens in the UK.

So what were these nonwovens?

Carefully selected mixtures of natural and man made fibres were blended in varying combinations according to the properties required in the finished fabric. The fibres were fed direct to the production line. A uniform fibre fleece was achieved by a special carding technique. The web produced was impregnated with synthetic latex foam and fed into the curing oven. When the web was thoroughly bonded, it was well washed and finishing processes were applied to achieve the qualities demanded, washability, hard or soft handling, etc.

The company was proud to be awarded the British Standards Institution BS 5750 (Part 2). The demand grew for Vilene Interlining, the best known product of its kind in

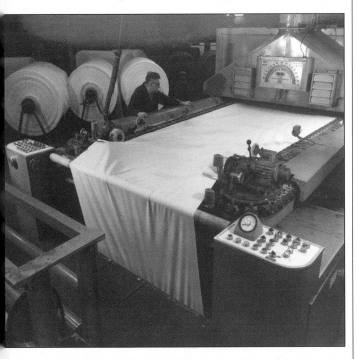

either the clothing industry and in home dressmaking. About this time, the Vilene Studio was formed to offer a unique technical advisory service. In the studio, clothing technicians checked all applications of Vilene before recommending it to a manufacturer. They were constantly at the disposal of the clothing industry.

Applications for the product were found outside the clothing industry. It was suitable for insulation materials in the electrical industry, filters for heating and ventilating, backing for PVC coating industry and interlining for shoes. It was used for the sound insulation of aircraft, for battery

separators, the manufacture of handbags and luggage and cleaning cloths. The company developed nylon based abrasive materials for household, industrial and catering use. They contributed to the production of protective suits for the armed forces for use at home and abroad against chemical and biological warfare and civilian protection against poisonous gases.

In 1970 the holding company had moved into electronics technology with computer accessories and printed circuit boards added to their product range.

Today, Freudenberg is a widely diversified international company, employing in the region of 26,000 people in 60 production plants in 22 countries.

Above: The staff canteen at the Greetland factory, circa 1965. This picture is included because it has a famous face on it!

Sitting at the table in the foreground, facing the camera is Gordon Kaye, star of the TV situation comedy 'Allo allo,' who worked for Bondina in the 1960s. Left: The Stenter Finishing Range. Right: An aerial view of the Greetland factory, which, because of its valley location, is almost invisible from the main roads.

A great company with a sound future based in Halifax

Mergers are nothing new to specialist motor insurer Bradford-Pennine which is now part of Royal & SunAlliance, the UK's largest general insurer.

Pennine Insurance was established in 1944 by a Halifax insurance broker to transact all classes of insurance with the exception of life insurance. Very quickly however, private car insurance became the specialist area of the company,

Fifteen years later in 1959 Bradford Insurance was founded as a diversification of the interests of the Tulketh Textile group. Originally intended to build a sound fire and accident portfolio centred on the Tulketh Headquarters at Peckover Street, Bradford, it rapidly began to win a competitive reputation in the life and motor insurance markets.

Even 30 years ago the problem of operational expenses suffered by smaller companies was evident and it is not surprising that both Bradford Insurance and Pennine insurance were searching for the same economies. They had much in common and the advantages of amalgamation became increasingly obvious.

Negotiations for the merger were completed in 1965 and whilst separate Head Offices were retained for a while, more and more processes were undertaken in Halifax.

Above: *This picture portrays the original house 'North Park' which lies to one corner of People's Park. The house and its gardens are now occupied by present offices of Bradford-Pennine Insurance. The picture was reproduced for a commemorative plate in 1987 when motor insurance policies exceeded one million in number.*
Left: *Dean Clough, home of Bradford-Pennine since 1944. This picture was taken circa 1900.*

Bradford-Pennine dedicated itself to business produced by insurance brokers and in 1965 dealt with 2,500 brokers, all of whom were authorised to sell motor insurance on a full credit basis.

Policyholders of the company grew from 175,000 to 257,000 in 1973 but the next few years were years of intense activity for Bradford-Pennine with the number of policyholders growing to 700,000 and premium income growing four fold to £31 m.

A number of changes were introduced to accommodate the expansion of the company including the centralisation of a dedicated claims office dealing with third party claims leaving the staff in the branch offices free to concentrate on the best possible service to the policyholder. Bradford-Pennine became a subsidiary of the Phoenix group, providing the company with appropriate capital to continue its expansion and achieve economics through effectiveness.

In August 1984 the Phoenix group merged with SunAlliance but Bradford-Pennine was largely unaffected operationally, although in the same year many of the staff were moved to premises in the newly refurbished offices at Bowling Mill, Dean Clough.

The company commemorated the sale of its one millionth motor insurance policy in 1987 by giving a special plate to all of its staff. The following year the company was awarded best Insurer of the Year by the institute of Insurance Brokers.

---

*Top: Dean Clough circa 1980. Since this picture was taken many changes have taken place at Dean Clough. Royal & SunAlliance occupies the building in the centre right of the picture, the same building that has always housed Bradford Pennine. **Above:** A 'Firemark'. These were used in the 17th and 18th centuries. Before the days of street names and numbers, insurance company Firemarks were attached to the outsides of buildings insured by them. Over time, the 'marks' acquired a subsidiary social function in that having insurance, and of course the choice of insurer, gave an indication of the owner's standing in society.*

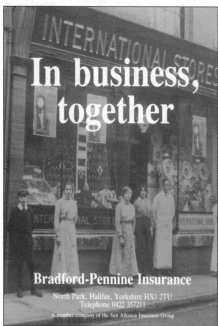

The dedication to the broker market was further confirmed in 1995 with the merger of the SunAlliance's broker household insurance business based in Oldham, giving the combined operation a greater range of products to offer its broker agents.

Further major change however was just around the corner when in 1996 SunAlliance and Royal Insurance merged to create the UK's largest general insurer - Royal & SunAlliance Group plc. Halifax has now become the Headquarters for the enlarged group's Personal Insurances, Broker Division encompassing Bradford-Pennine and expanding within the Dean Clough premises. Headed by Tim Ablett, previously Chief Executive of Bradford-Pennine, the business, in addition to its headquarters in Halifax, now includes national centres in Oldham, Liverpool, Glasgow, Maidstone and a specialist unit in London. The newly merged operation retains its focus on the broker and intermediary market and now boasts premium income of some £450m, 1,800 staff and over 10,000 brokers and agents selling its motor and household products.

With today's consumers faced with such an overwhelming choice of policies and variety of sales channels from which to acquire those policies it is important that insurance companies are focused and provide exceptional customer service. This is a key aim at Royal & SunAlliance where the goal is to be their customers' first choice.

Above: This nostalgic advertisement was run in the 1980s. The shop shown was one of those insured by Bradford Pennine in its infancy.
Top: The laying of the foundation stones of the new offices at North Park in the 1970s.
Right: A compliment slip dating from the 1970s.

with compliments

Bradford-Pennine Insurance Group

NORTH PARK
HALIFAX
HX1 2TU

Telephone: Halifax 63031

Bradford Insurance Company Limited
The Pennine Insurance Company Limited

Registered Office: North Park · Halifax · HX1 2TU
Registered at London England with numbers 165018 (Bradford Insurance Company Limited) and
391937 (The Pennine Insurance Company Limited).

SunAlliance's origins date back to the foundation of the Sun Insurance office in London in 1710. Royal & SunAlliance has strong connections with two of Britain's great historic seaports outside of London- Liverpool where Royal Insurance has its roots back in 1845 and Bristol where Phoenix Assurance was established in 1782.

Doubtless this is what led Royal & SunAlliance to sponsor yachtswoman Tracy Edwards and her all female crew, which on 1 July 1997 set a new record in their catamaran 'Royal & SunAlliance" for the fastest all female crew to sail across the Atlantic. The record was established in nine days, eleven hours and twenty two minutes.

Above: When the new offices were completed, Bradford-Pennine were fortunate to have them officially opened by HRH Prince Charles, The Prince of Wales.

Top: Tim Ablett, Director of Personal Insurances - Royal & SunAlliance.

Left: The giant 92 foot catamaran **Royal & SunAlliance,** skippered by Tracy Edwards (far right) as it crossed the Atlantic in record speed in July 1997.

West Vale - home of the worlds' favourite airline blankets!

Left: A letterhead dating from the 1940s. *Below:* Early transportation methods! This picture dates from the turn of the century and shows how bales and raw material were moved around.

M any Halifax folk will be aware of the firm John Horsfall & Sons Limited of West Vale. With well over a century of history behind it, the company has a proud connection with the area. The company was established in 1863 and began with a partnership between James Clay and John Horsfall. The company was then known as Clay & Horsfall (which incidentally has no connection with the later company of the same name in Sowerby Bridge).

The early days
John Horsfall was a plumber and builder by trade so it was a step in a strange direction when he founded the company which manufactured blankets. Luddenden Foot was its first home and it remained so until 1872 when it moved to Sowerby Bridge, into rented premises at Clough Works in Gratrix Lane.

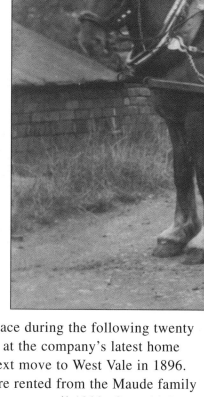

Further moves took place during the following twenty years and a major fire at the company's latest home was followed by its next move to West Vale in 1896. The premises here were rented from the Maude family for the first seven years up until 1903 after which time they were bought. These premises were the only home of John Horsfall for a hundred years until the company bought 'Victoria Works', an additional factory in Elland for finishing purposes, in 1996.

Left: Whiteley Horsfall (left), John Horsfall, the company's founder (centre), John William Horsfall (right).
Right: A line drawing of the Horsfall West Vale works from the early 1900s.

'Dog-Tags'

A system was introduced very early on which alleviated the confusion which could have arisen due to the sheer numbers of men who were there day-by-day. Wages were given by number. Each man wore a 'dog-tag' around his neck and at the end of the week when wages were due, his number would be called and he would go to the office to receive his pay.

A family company

In 1871 John's eldest son, Whiteley joined the company and following soon afterwards his second son, John William

The wars years

The First World War saw increased activity for the company with their products being requisitioned for the war effort, although it also saw many of its workforce going to the front to fight. John William died in 1922 after which the third son, Percy took control. Percy died in 1938, leaving the business, as were many at the time, in a state much bruised by the difficult years of trading in the 1930s. It is worthy of note that the three brothers of the second generation had guided the destiny of the company for a total of 52 years. *Continued overleaf*

became involved. The company initially specialised in all kinds of wool processing, originally on various wool and cotton types.

The founder ran the company after the partnership between James Clay and himself was dissolved, changing the name to John Horsfall & Co until his death in 1886. From this time until his own untimely death in 1905 Whiteley ran the company after which John William took over the reins.

From previous page
Percy only had a daughter so it was left to his son-in-law, Arthur Benson to pick up the reins.

During the Second World War, John Horsfall's made very large quantities of blankets for the Admiralty who, in contrast to all other services and even at the height of the conflict, used only the very best blankets of the whitest wools. Added to these were a very heavy wool cloth called 'Fearnought', made in all for over 100 years and which was used for lining ammunition boxes and had also been used for caulking holes in the hulls of wooden ships! This cloth is still today used for firefighting suits.

In the aftermath of war there was a time of insatiable demand for blankets which helped the company to recover from the pre-war depression and later to become the only blanket manufacturing survivor in the Halifax area, which had about ten producers before the war.

In the fourth generation, Arthur's son, John Horsfall W Benson, who joined the company in 1951 is now the chairman and his son, Peter Horsfall Benson, who was appointed managing director in May 1997, is the fifth generation from the founder.

The present.....
The company's markets are world wide with 60% of products being exported to most parts of the globe, particularly to the far East, Australasia, North America, Europe and the middle East. Also, closer to home, British Airways is one of

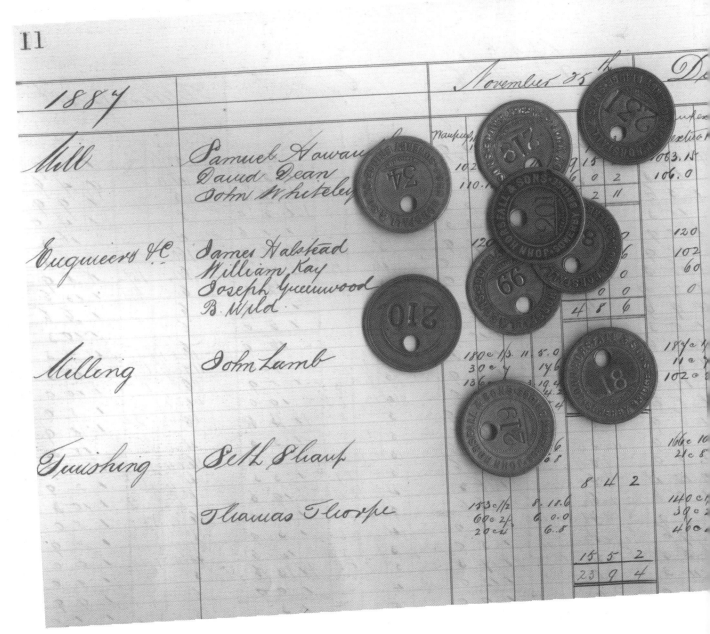

John Horsfall's biggest customers. In fact, some sixty airlines are supplied with blankets from this Halifax company.

Quality and safety are the principal features governing production and John Horsfall blankets are fire retardant, comfortable and durable, in various weights, designs and sizes. The work is carried out by a highly skilled and dedicated workforce, who work with the very latest in production equipment.

Perhaps surprisingly, the company's main competitors are based in Europe and many of its blankets are supplied to the United States airlines for use in their Premium, Business and First Class cabins.

....and the future

The world's airline business is expanding at a rate of 5 to 10% per year. Meeting this increasing demand features largely in John Horsfall's plans besides the additional customers who also come to the company for their requirements. Whilst the company continues to manufacture traditional bed blankets, comparatively few of these are bought by retail outlets for home use, so the company is tending to direct its attention towards hotels and cruiselines.

John Horsfall & Sons Limited is proud of its long association with Halifax and the surrounding area, employing local skilled people with long traditions of weaving. Only sheer hard work, dedication and quality has led the company to its present position, and only the same will see it through into the next millennium.

Above left: Percy Horsfall, third son of the founder of the company and who ran the company for sixteen years until his death in 1938.

Above: An aerial view of West Vale dating from 1931. The John Horsfall and Son Ltd factory can be seen in the lower part of the photograph.

Left: A copy of an early wages ledger, with examples of the 'dog tags' used by the men to identify them for wages purposes.

Below: John Horsfalls engine house using a pair of Compound Corliss Condensing Engines made by Wood Brothers of Sowerby Bridge and widely used by the wool processing industry. This one dates from 1903.

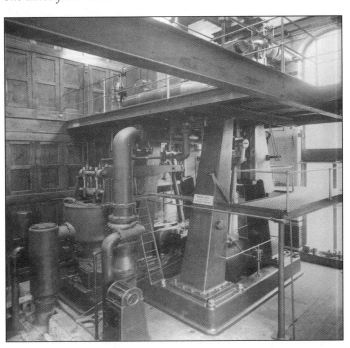

Halifax - home of the world's tastiest sweets
From the Mackintosh days to the new Nestlé era

In 1890, Violet Mackintosh opened a home made cake shop in King Cross Lane in Halifax. She was a good baker and the little venture prospered. Her husband, John, meanwhile was foreman in a silk mill. However, he was a partner in his wife's business and continually invented new lines to add to the range of scones, tea cakes and parkin. She experimented with sweet making and managed to produce a toffee that was different.

Working at nights, the couple produced just a few batches of the toffee to sell on Saturdays only. A few days prior to the introduction of this new venture, John put a bill in the shop window. "Mackintosh's Celebrated Toffee. Come and eat at our expense!" He understood his fellow Yorkshiremen!

The following week another bill told them they had tasted at the shop's expense and now they would have to taste at their own. Soon, Violet could no longer cope with the demand when she had cakes to bake as well. John decided to give up his mill work and join her in the toffee business.

They produced more of it than could be sold in the shop, so John went 'on the road' to other small shops in Halifax, He borrowed £50 for a horse and cart, though he hated debt. Some of the Mackintosh relatives were brought into the busi-

ness and, in spite of some temporary setbacks they all prospered. A move was made from King Cross Lane to a small rented factory. By 1898, he had managed to put aside £11,000. He needed to borrow a further £4,000 to build his own factory in Queens Road and his first priority was to pay off this debt. Sales spread throughout Yorkshire, then throughout the UK.

From the very beginning, John Mackintosh put aside a small percentage of the takings for advertising. When the North Pole was reached for the first time, Mackintosh's poster showed a tin of toffees in the snow there with a caption that read, 'If you can't get Mackintosh's toffee in your neighbourhood, leave the neighbourhood!'

Leaving relatives to produce and sell at home, John travelled, looking for new markets. As early as 1902, he had factories in the USA and Germany. In 1908, he was joined by his eldest son, Harold , but in 1914 the two eldest boys volunteered to defend their country, Harold in the Navy and Douglas in the army, despite Douglas being under-age. John spent the time preparing to extend the business when the war finished. However, it was not to be. John died suddenly, at the early age of 51, in 1920, within a year of his sons rejoining him.

When the Queens Road factory burnt down in November 1911, the company moved to Albion Mills immediately. Queens Road was rebuilt as a chocolate factory and Harold Mackintosh was sent to Germany to learn chocolate making. A.J. Caley in Norwich was taken over in 1932 and John's third son, Eric was sent there as managing director. Harold Mackintosh was chairman from 1921 until his death in November 1964.

Above: On Friday March 20th 1931 the Daily Dispatch carried this advertisement for Mackintosh's Carnival Assortment. 'You can pick and choose to your palate's content' customers were told. Above right: John Mackintosh, founder of the company at his desk with his eldest son - later to become Viscount Mackintosh.

now had the Mackintosh label. The Caley name was not phased out until the 1960s.

On the 8th June 1941 the firm's 50th anniversary was celebrated. Because the date John Mackintosh's business was established was uncertain, he chose the date of the birth of his first son, so that the company celebration coincided with Harold's 50th birthday. Harold was presented with a book signed by every employee.

By the 1960s, Harold Mackintosh had been made a Viscount and Douglas and Eric were joint managing directors of the firm. Douglas's sons, Peter and Martin, joined the business as development engineer and chartered accountant respectively.

In 1969 John Mackintosh and Sons Ltd. merged with Rowntree to become Rowntree- Mackintosh.

By 1988, Rowntree Mackintosh had been acquired by Nestlé. The Halifax site currently employs in the region of twelve hundred people in the production of Toffo, Quality Street, Walnut Whip and Easter Eggs. It is a far cry from the little shop opened by the formidable lady in her deeply fringed shawl. She had died in 1932. After her death, a parcel was found, labelled 'Never to be opened. Of course, her surviving relatives did open it. Inside, they found Violet and John's marriage certificate, Violet's certificate as a Sunday school teacher and the original toffee recipe. The little collection represented the principles on which she based her life and the principles on which the company she and John founded has been run.

Mackintosh's was one of the first firms in England to set up a health service for their employees. It benefited the management too, since skin diseases are dangerous in a food factory and bad teeth do not help hygiene. There was no NHS and most employees did have skin and teeth problems. One shilling a week bought health care, including dentistry, at the firm's expense.

The Mackintosh range of confectionery was boosted in 1935 with the launch of Rolo, joined a year later in 1936 by Quality Street, which gained its name from J.M. Barrie's play. Chocolate and toffee were used together for the first time in Quality Street, which, at that time was said to be an expensive product, priced at sixpence a quarter pound.

When forty five shillings was the average factory wage, it would take two hours to earn enough to buy one pound. Nowadays, at about £3 for a pound, it would take only about

Top left: The Mackintosh's Sand competition in August 1922. The picture (made in sand) was a reproduction of ML Attwell's picture 'The Fairies' toffee town.' **Above right:** *A wartime advertisement.*
Left: A delivery wagon dating from the 1930s. **Below:** *'The largest toffee manufacturer in the world', proclaimed the advertisement that accompanied this line drawing.*

forty minutes.

1939 brought war once more and in 1942 the Caley factories were completely destroyed. The fabric had gone but the initiative remained to make the rebuilt factory the most modern chocolate making plant in the world. The Caley label was still used for exports but the chocolate sold in the UK

Halifax firm fans the flames of progress

Since its inception Halifax Fan Limited has been a dedicated fan manufacturer specialising in the design and manufacture of centrifugal fans, with the product range increasing over the years. Established in 1965 to serve local industry, the company now supplies most industries throughout the world from its four acre manufacturing site in Halifax.

From its humble beginnings in a former debtors' prison in Gaol Lane to the present day, throughout the company's growth and development Halifax Fan has remained firmly rooted in the community from which it takes its name. Right from the start, every one of its products has been designed, developed and built in Halifax and everything originates from the company's own designs.

The company was founded by Mr. David A. Scott, a mechanical engineer who specialised in ductwork design and ventilating systems, together with two colleagues, Brian Walker and Roy Taylor, who became directors. Additional assistance from Mr. Scott's mother provided them with secretarial and general administration services. Later this role was taken on by Mr. Scott's wife, Mary, who assisted her husband for many years - she also painted the walls when the company made its first move to Grantham

Road, Haley Hill, having doubled its workforce and outgrown the Gaol Lane premises within its first year.

Throughout the 1970s and much of the Eighties the major challenge facing Halifax Fan was meeting customer demand and coping with the sheer volume of an ever-expanding order book. (It was during this period that the present managing director, Charles Rodley, joined the company.)

The resultant growth of the company led to a further move in 1972 to Halifax Fan's present Mistral Works site at Salterhebble, and continued development has seen the manufacturing facility extended four times and three office expansions, increasing the whole area by three-and-a-half-times its original size.

Halifax Fan invests heavily in the training and development of its staff and a planned apprentice training scheme ensures not only a constant supply of highly skilled production staff, but also a strong and very experienced engineering and management team. Many of today's senior personnel originally joined the company as apprentices or in other junior positions.

First class production resources have always been of prime importance and in the years since 1965 the company's manufacturing machinery and equipment has developed from oxyacetylene cutters, a set of rollers and a hand bender to the present state-of-the-art £1/4m laser-cutting machine. The resulting precision means that components are so accurately made that they can be assembled rather than fitted during final fan construction; no hammering is required to make things fit.

An ongoing programme of investment ensures that Halifax Fan maintains its position as a leader in its field. Computerisation was taken on board at a very early stage, led by David Scott who initially took a computer home and worked at it until he was sufficiently

Above: A Halifax Bomber which was used by Halifax Fan in a 1980s advert.
Left: A late 1970s advert for the company.

who currently do not fully appreciate exactly what Halifax Fan has to offer.

Managing director Charles Rodley sums up the company's mission as follows: "To make the best fans in the world, satisfying individual customer specifications, so that they instinctively turn to Halifax Fan for all their fan requirements."

Although Halifax Fan's founder, David Scott, retired in 1996 he still retains an active interest in the company in his advisory capacity as Consultant. And the Scott family connection is also maintained through David's son Jonathan who joined the company after qualifying as a mechanical engineer and is now a Technical Sales Engineer out 'on the road.'

competent to write his first programme for fan selection. Today, not only are detailed specifications produced by computer, but production is controlled via a sophisticated CAD/CAM system linked from the Design Office directly to the laser cutting machine.

Above: The founder of the company, David Scott (left) with the works manager, John Meehan. in 1974.
Below: An aerial view of the firm's Salterhebble works, showing the familiar curve of Salterhebble Hill on the left.

Fans manufactured are high quality heavy duty centrifugal fans, incorporating a unique design of bearing assembly. They are rigorously tested and very accurately balanced for smooth operation and long wear life. To ensure that every fan is suited to its intended application, customer requirements are calculated carefully from the operational specification supplied. All fan ranges are tested to BS848, thereby guaranteeing performance.

It is this dedication to detail which has resulted in Halifax Fan's excellent reputation world-wide for quality and reliability and which saw the company at the forefront of fan manufacturers in being certificated, in 1986, to the then prestigious, and now essential, BS5750 Part 1 (now BS EN ISO 9001) Quality Assurance Standard.

The company's extensive customer list represents a comprehensive range of market sectors and applications, major areas being in the process control industries, food, chemical and, of course, dust control in foundries and quarries. Many fans are also destined for overseas locations, more often than not incorporated into machines or process plants manufactured by Halifax Fan's own customers.

Future plans include expansion of the customer base to encompass the many potential customers

McVities Cake Company, continuing a proud baking tradition

History of the Halifax Factory

The factory, now 86 years old, began life in 1907 as Riley's sweet factory. The Riley brothers started their business in their own house, moving to Hopwood Lane in 1911. Their business remained independent for over half a century before it was purchased by the Guinness group who sold out later to Callard and Bowser. Finally, in 1988, came the sale of Callard and Bowser to United Biscuits, and with it the factory.

History of the Cake Company

McVitie's have a strong cake baking heritage. In 1923 they had the honour of baking the Queen Mother's Wedding cake and subsequently many of the Royal family's celebration cakes into the 1940s. Around this time, cake production was set up at the company's factory in Harlesden, London, to take advantage of the distribution benefits afforded by the Grand Union Canal.

In the 1960s, it was United Biscuit's company Chairman, Sir Hector Laing's, aim to make McVitie's the lowest cost

capitalise on this, the Cake Company was set up in 1989 a an independent business unit, with its own dedicated management team. This development brought with it an increased focus on innovation, leading to the launch of Jamaica Ginger, Golden Syrup, Jaffa and Penguin cake bars. The individually wrapped cake bar sector, pioneered by McVitie's, remains even now the fastest growing sector in the total ambient cake market.

The unprecedented success of these new products meant that a new manufacturing facility had to be established, and so the company moved to its new site in Halifax.

producer of bar cakes. He achieved this, helped by the high-tech automation at Harlesden, where production was centralised during the 1970s, alongside the biscuit factory. Business at that time focused on long-life products, such as bar cakes, fruit cake and traditional Christmas cakes, and benefited from shared distribution costs with the biscuit factory.

The 1980s brought new opportunities. Better transport facilities and a move away from home baking towards a more convenient lifestyle resulted in increased business for McVitie's Cake Company and increased profits. To

Why Halifax?

Going north was the best move for the company to make for many reasons. Not only did the move mean a significant reduction in overhead costs, but also the situation of Halifax near to the M1, M62 and M6 offered obvious benefits for distribution. The factory in Hopwood Lane was chosen partly because there was room for expansion but, more importantly, because the Managing Director of the Cake Company was so impressed by the fine record of production that the team of people on site had achieved, despite a recession and far from modern equipment.

Far left: An early letterhead.
Left: The Queen Mother's wedding cake, baked by McVities in 1923.
Above: An early photograph of the Riley's sweet factory in Hopwood Lane, Halifax - later to become the Halifax home of McVities Cakes.

in 1994/5 and by a further 20% in the following year, fuelled largely by the launch of the Go Ahead! brand, including a range of individually wrapped cake bars which are up to 97% fat free!

'Having our future in our own hands is a great incentive,' says the managing director. 'We will be able to get things done fast and, with the team of people we have at Halifax we expect to really go places.'

Above: Women workers from the 1920s packing Riley's Rum & Butter Dainties at the Hopwood Lane factory.
Left: The offices of Riley's Sweets during the 1920s. Clerks would stand at the desks on the right of the picture, completing the large ledgers in pen and ink.
Below: The present day Halifax factory - now at the forefront of modern baking technology

The Halifax work force had misgivings about the drastic changes this takeover brought for them and embarked on their retraining reluctantly. They had to work on three shifts where they had previously worked strictly days. They soon came round as the new company promised them security and expansion. The 300 strong staff of 1973 had been whittled to 150 but the changes immediately necessitated 60 new jobs with the expectation of many more. McVitie's investment of £5 million, and the fact that their factory had become not just a satellite but the management centre for United Biscuits' expanding cake company, was very reassuring.

Success followed the move. The number of employees has increased in the last five years by 67% and production has continued to expand. Company growth increased by 18%

Holset, a firm with over twenty five years of success in Halifax

The company was formed in 1952 as a member of the BHD group of companies in Turnbridge, Huddersfield. The company name comes from the name of W.C. HOLmes company and the founding designer and first Managing Director, Louis CroSET.

Louis Croset was a Swiss engineer who designed the world's first ever flexible coupling in 1936 and joined the WC Holmes company to manufacture them. Flexible couplings for connecting rotating shafts and viscous dampers for reducing torsional vibration in engine crankshafts were the companies original product range.

Paul Croset, the son of Louis Croset took over the running of the company in the early 1950s and it grew rapidly during that decade, supplying prestigious diesel engine manufacturers like Rolls Royce and Sulzer and all the major Steel Works throughout England. Turbochargers were added to the product range in 1957 and fan drives were soon to follow. By 1965 the company had grown significantly employing nearly 800 people and was rapidly running out of space to expand at the Huddersfield site.

In 1973, the company was acquired by the American diesel engine manufacturer Cummins Engine Co. and expansion plans created the need to relocate part of the business. Halifax was chosen as the best site heavily influenced by the high grade of skilled people in the area. In 1973 Fan drive manufacture was transferred from Huddersfield. In the spring of 1974 people from the Halifax area were hired for training in the production processes at Huddersfield for the next wave of plant transfer that was soon to follow.

In the annual summer shut down of 1974 a massive effort was undertaken to transfer all the machine tools which manufactured the company's flexible couplings and viscous vibration dampers, to Halifax. The management team overseeing the transfer and early years of production were Ron Hesselden, Site Director and Roy Holt, Plant Manager.

Above: A 1950s photograph showing Holset engineers at work, testing the torsional dampers for the 'Deltic' diesel train engine.
Left: Holset also made the torsional dampers for this type of locomotive in the 1960s.
Above right: Famous steeplejack Fred Dibnah's traction engine made an appearance at a Holset 'open day' some years ago.
Right: Receiving the plaque of appreciation from the President of Hyundai for exemplary support.

The new premises were on the former site of Churchill Redman machine tools in the West End area of Halifax. Twenty of the former employees of Churchill Redman were among the first new staff in Halifax. Prior to Churchill Redman the site had been a casting foundry to the railway industry. The site was known as Longfield works.

Initially there were 26 people employed on site and at the company's peak in Halifax there were over 360 people. It was not until the Christmas of 1980 that the full complement of technical and commercial support departments were relocated to the Halifax site. The quality of people and team spirit within the workforce has always been a strong point in the favour of the Halifax site. At the annual inter-plant sports days the much smaller workforce at Halifax had a David and Goliath task to beat the Huddersfield plant in competition. The team spirit within the company was extended to families, friends and the wider community with regular Company Open Days. At the open days Design, Development and Production areas would be demonstrated to show people what it was that 'Dad and Mum' spent all their time doing during the day as well as competitions and exhibits of trucks and machines where the company products were used as well as displays by the suppliers.

People training and a quality focus from the beginning were foundations of the companies success. Numerous Quality awards have been obtained from companies like, Ford, Volvo, Jaguar and British Rail and in June 1991 Holset was one of the first companies in the Calderdale area to be accredited with the international quality standard ISO 9001 by Lloyds Register.

Over 70% of the sales from Halifax have been exported to every corner of the world. Notable orders were obtained to supply flexible couplings for pumping stations on the trans-Siberian pipe line in 1975. The Halifax Lord Mayor's office bears a photo of a Canadian Frigate called "The Halifax". This was presented to the mayor by Canadian Naval officers following orders Holset won to supply couplings on the propulsion system for the Canadian naval fleet of vessels.

Following the Oil crisis of the late seventies ship owners started to replace oil-fired steam engines with more fuel efficient diesel engines. This led to a great demand for the companies 3 metre diameter viscous dampers weighing over 15 tons. A prestigious plaque of appreciation was received from the President of Hyundai for exemplary support to Hyundai in Korea. Holset was the only supplier in the world who could design and supply the products to solve their technical problems. Holset is one of the few British companies to supply automotive products into Japan due to the superior quality of the company's viscous dampers.

In Published technical design manuals on torsional vibration the expertise of Holset is recognised and all authors refer to the 'Holset Damper' as the generic term for Viscous Dampers like the general public say 'Hoover' for vacuum cleaners.

A restructuring of the Holset group in recent times has resulted in sales of the coupling business to Renold Plc in June 1996 and the expertise of the torsional vibration damper business was acquired by Simpson Industries, Inc in July 1997. Investment in the latest laser welding technology for manufacture of viscous dampers for the truck market is keeping Simpson Industries at the forefront of the race for competitiveness in the supply of components to world markets from Halifax.

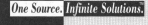 One Source. *Infinite Solutions.*™

 SIMPSON INDUSTRIES

Sagar Richards - engineering excellence on a worldwide scale

Sagar Richards Ltd was first incorporated as a Limited Company on July 12th 1919, the initial shareholders being Henry Sagar, Daniel Richards and Alfred Richards. The first company secretary (later to become managing director) was Henry Rutter, who retired from the company in 1966. Premises were leased at Woodbottom Works in Luddendenfoot and the company remained there until 1962. Henry Sagar and Henry Rutter were in charge throughout the late 1920s and early 1930s and were joined by Charles Norwood, who together saw the company rise to relative prosperity in the late 1930s through to the 1940s. Henry Sagar died in 1947 but his fellow directors continued until the 1960s.

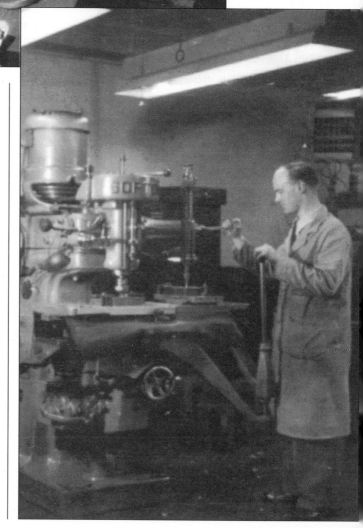

Top: For most of its history Sagar Richards has produced castings by the gravity method. Over the years the shape and complexity of the dies has changed along with the variation of product. In this picture from the 1950s, two casters are seen tilting the die, whilst the pourer pours the metal into the ingate area. Bottom: Another 1950s picture showing the slow and labour intensive process of the machining of heat resistant die. It was into these dies that the molten metal was poured.

Initial production at Woodbottom works was of castings in aluminium and zinc alloys but in the mid 1920s Aluminium Bronze (AB) was developed by the company as a casting alloy. It was with this alloy that the company developed as a significant local supplier to the British motor trade and more recently the worldwide motor trade. In the late 1920s the company experienced severe financial difficulties resulting in pay cuts for the workforce. The company was on the verge of being wound up but was able to come to an arrangement with its creditors whereby they accepted shares in the company for the amounts owed to them instead of cash.

The reorganisation resulted in a change in the company's fortunes and, as well as obtaining orders for vacuum cleaner parts, orders were also received from the British motor industry including Riley Engines, Morris Commercial Cars and many other well-known companies of the day.

Progress was slow but steady and by the mid 1930s the creditor shareholders were beginning to see a return on their investment, however late it may have seemed. However, the company faced stiff competition from Aluminium Bronze Co Ltd, the major part of whose business was absorbed by Sagar Richards in 1980.

A boost was given to the company when Rover was added to the client list in 1937 and when the Second World War came the company had to operate a three shift system working seven days a week to produce aluminium valves holders for gas masks in addition to other products. A bomb shelter was erected by the company to accommodate 198 people and, in order to secure power supplies, an area of ground at Luddendenfoot

Railway Station was rented as a reserve coal storage place.

In 1942 the company introduced a Joint Production Consultative and Advisory Committee, which consisted of half management and half employees. The workers represented the Foundry, Toolroom and Trimming Shop. Cooper House Mills Weaving Shed was acquired as a machine shop in 1943 and in the same year bonuses were introduced for chargehands and tool setters. This was related to piecework earnings.

Henry Sagar reached his 80th birthday in 1945 and died two years later in 1947. He was succeeded as chairman by his son, Lawrence who occupied this position until 1972.

The end of the war saw a down-turn in production for government contracts but with business still generally buoyant, the problems of labour shortage and the desire for improved premises were apparent. Consideration was given to relocation to Newcastle and Jarrow, although after many visits to these areas the company decided to stay in Yorkshire and to make better use of the existing facilities.

Although the company was successful, it saw the need, in 1950 for improvement and hired

consultants to raise the efficiency of the work flow, to improve inspection at all stages and to reduce scrap, thereby increasing the potential of the Foundry and Machine Shop. Property was purchased in 1955 in which offices were built and the Synchro Works (now the Forge) was built in 1958.

In 1958 the company considered going 'public' but this never materialised as it was purchased by F Francis & Sons (Holdings) Ltd, later to become Francis Industries Ltd.

The first production supplies of AB Synchroniser Rings to the Ford Motor Company began in 1959, to be quickly followed by Selector Fork enquiries later the same year.
contd overleaf

Above: A view of New Mill before the current Calderside Works was built. The picture dates from roughly 1958 - 1959. In the foreground is the current training room which was then the accounts/wages department and was the scene of the fire in 1973.
Left: The Certificate of Incorporation was given to the company on 12th July 1919, in recognition of the fact that the company had gained limited liability status. Below: Nearly complete, the current Calderside Works. This new building was fully utilised in 1963.

side needed strengthening to avoid water seepage into the new Machine Shop.

The company became exclusive suppliers of AB Selector Forks to Ford and the level of this business was at its peak with demand also high for AB Synchroniser Rings. However the threat from high tensile brass for synchroniser rings was becoming more apparent.

In 1965, after long negotiations, a German company agreed to supply Sagar-Richards with the technical 'know-how' and support to manufacture brass synchroniser rings. By 1966, supplies of brass Synchroniser Rings from Germany were being machined by Sagar Richards prior to being delivered to Ford. By the following year AB rings were phased out as brass ring production took precedence.

With the financial benefits of being part of a Group, the New Mill was bought from Whitworth and Co, together with a group of local cottages known as 'Narrow Nick'. These premises were demolished in 1961 and the transfer to the new Calderside Works, as they became known, was completed the following year and the Woodbottom site was vacated.

Further developments took place over the following five years, allowing for growth and greater efficiency. By 1973 the company began to diversify into other products such as

Above: A Civic visit on 31st January 1977. Demonstrating the procedures is Wilf Smith whilst being watched by the Mayor of Calderdale, Cllr Mrs Mona Mitchell and her consort, Mr Reg Mitchell JP. **Right:** *Advances in automation provided the company with the latest generation of machine. Today, Autoload CNC Machine Lathes manufacture Synchroniser Rings and they are measured by CNC co-ordinate Measuring Machines.*

The old mill at Cooper House was demolished in 1963 and the new Machine Shop was in use by 1964. During the building work, negotiations with the Rochdale Canal Company started as the canal

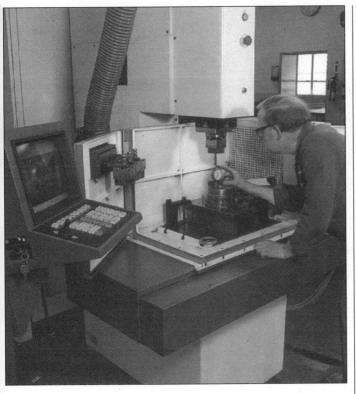

alloy car wheels and golf putters, as well as early experimentation with the shell moulding of iron. None of these ideas really took off. However, the shell moulding did begin later.

The majority of the administration offices were destroyed by fire in 1973, following an explosion caused by a gas cylinder. The accident had occurred when heaters were being moved. One toppled over and loosened the control valve. The heater was dragged towards the door when the cylinder suddenly exploded and blasted out one side of the office block. Mr Schofield (the unfortunate man who had been carrying the cylinder) escaped with a slight finger injury and very singed hair whilst the other members of staff managed to climb out of the windows and were therefore unhurt. The remnants of this building are now used as a training room.

In order to provide space at Cooper House for the new Shell Moulding Factory, an old textile mill about a quarter of a mile away, called Holme Royd Mill was purchased in 1974 to house the Machine Shop. This remained until 1991 when, as part of a rationalisation programme, it was vacated and the Machine Shop was returned to Cooper House. Holme Royd Mill was demolished in 1995.

Around the mid 1970s forays were made to the USA to find additional sales outlets. The first of these was Michigan Export Co (now known as Tremec) for AB Selector Forks and later for brass Synchroniser Rings. This was a foothold into the USA leading to significant orders. Yorkshire Engineering Supplies Ltd of Leeds was acquired in 1981 but was closed down in 1983 with all activities from this company being transferred to Cooper House.

During the 1980s the company concentrated on becoming an international supplier of brass synchroniser rings, with a client list that included Chrysler and Volvo and later that decade Mazda of Japan. Fiat and Renault joined the list in the early 1990s.

Moving on to today, advances in automation have provided the company with the latest generation of machines. In summary a sound business venture which began in the 1930s and was built up until the 1960s on the strength of its Aluminium Bronze alloy, but it is now concentrating on brass Synchroniser Rings. It is also a business which recognises that things change with time, moving with the flow to maintain its growth and remain the best in its field within the automotive industry

Top left: The latest CNC spark eroder which eliminates the need for hand polishing when the spark erosion is complete. The machine is capable of extremely fine finishes.
Left: An aerial view of the Calderside site, taken in the early 1990s.

Success over adversity at Farrar Brushes

James Farrar Brushes was established in 1870 and was then known as Stannery Brush Works of Halifax, West Yorkshire. The company was run by two brothers for a while but eventually they dissolved the partnership and split up. Both brothers remained in the brush manufacturing industry. James Farrar moved his business to the present location in 1904, into a purpose built factory at Spring Hall Lane, Halifax. In those days a large majority of the work came from the local cotton and woollen mills around Yorkshire and Lancashire. Farrar brushes were used for all purposes in this industry; from small ones for cleaning the more awkward parts of the machine to huge brushes which cleaned off slubs as cloth was passed over them.

The company employed around fifteen to twenty people at the turn of the century, in various kinds of occupation. For instance there were the old pitch pans in the cellar for making heavy industrial sweeping brooms and small hand brushes which went into the mills, breweries and local councils.

Another type of work was hand drawing. This consisted of looping bristles through the wire frame and pulling it through holes, to give a stitched effect. Provided this was done right, there was no chance of the bristles falling out and because of this these brushes were used in the food industry. The third type of brush made at Farrars are the twisted-in-wire brushes. These are used for cleaning boilers, condenser tubes, chimneys and all types of bottles. There are thousands of designs of brushes made in this way in all sorts of shapes and sizes. Most people will have an example of twisted-in-wire work in their homes in the shape of bottle brushes.

Exports

During the 1930s Farrars looked overseas to expand their market and for the next three decades much of the work produced was exported, the majority of which was twisted-in-wire brushes which had proved most successful and reliable over the years.

The current managing director, Kenneth Crossley joined the company in 1961 after doing National Service with the Royal Air Force. At this time things were changing. The textile industry was on the decline and all around Yorkshire and Lancashire mills were closing down. The pitching pan department which produced the heavier brushes was closed and over the next few years the company had to enforce a three-day week, whilst a lot of companies in the same type of industry were going out of business.

Specialisation

The firm soon realised that it had to specialise in just one or two types of brushes rather that attempt to dabble in everything. As time went by the work dried up more and more and as people left the company they weren't replaced. It was indeed a bleak time.

In 1984, the company secretary at that time fell ill and had retirement forced upon him. George Montague Booth was the nephew of the founder, James Farrar and had run the business almost single handed for fifty years before his illness. This meant that the work was left to just three people. The two directors of the company were Mr Farrar's daughters (who at this time were in their eighties). They were aided by Ken Crossley but for obvious reasons they decided to sell up.

Ken and his wife decided to take a chance and purchase the firm. It was a risk, as the business was barely breaking even at the time and over the years following this decision the couple have faced many problems. The road hasn't been easy and Ken would probably be the first to admit this. However, the company is still here, almost a hundred years after its humble beginnings and is doing well.

A proud family business, with two sons, Ian and Jonathan and the couple's daughter, Jacqueline work for the company which now specialises in twisted-in-wire brushed. The work carried out is interesting and varied and the directors of the company feel sure that the business, despite its problems of the past, will carry on into its bi-centenary and beyond.

Top left: A line drawing of the Spring Hall Lane factory.
Left: A 1960s advert for the firms specialist brushes.
Below: The Spring Hall Lane works as it is today.

This sporting life

consolation for Halifax though, their cut of the Wembley gate receipts was over £1800. This was not to be the last taste of Wembley for Halifax's Rugby League followers; much success was achieved by the local team in the 1950s, but that is another story...

Above: The 1948-49 Halifax R.L.F.C team which succeeded in reaching the Wembley Final. The team played Bradford Northern but the event was less than momentous for Halifax, who failed to score in the match and became the first team in the history of Wembley Finals not to score there or even get a shot at goal. there was a financial

Below: A lesser nostalgia book writer would have been confused by this picture, for it features a mixture of Halifax Town Soccer players and Halifax Rugby League players. It relates to a time when players from each discipline would play a charity match against other - one half rugby and one half soccer. The Halifax Rugby League players are wearing white shorts with the broad band across the middle. Some familiar names from the world of of local rugby are present. From left to right on the back row are Len Holsen, Frank Mawson, Ken Dean, Dennis Bradley, Ken Ward, Mike Condon, and, behind them, in the goal keepers jersey, Ken Dean. Crouching, in the middle, is Lou Falcon. On the front row, kneeling, is Ted Brakes (soccer), Terry Cook, Arthur Daniels, Jack Schofield and Stan Kielty.

Bird's eye view

Surely one of the most fascinating photographs in the whole of this book, an aerial view of Halifax which was taken on a sunny day in 1949. The first impression given by the picture is how dark all the buildings looked in those pre-smoke-controlled days. Many of the town's best-known monuments can be seen clearly in the picture, but they look brighter now thanks to a determined effort to get them cleaned up in the late 1960s and early 1970s. The top right of the scene contains the many factories and mills once located in this part of Halifax, along with the distinctive cooling towers and power station. Woolshops, before it was redeveloped of course, with the Tudor building and Driver's store at the head of it, joins Northgate. Further towards the centre of the scene the white facade of Burton's building is visible. Broad Street, on the left of the picture, is shown mid-way through its development; The Odeon Cinema was well established in 1949 (it had been opened in 1938) but the land behind it, destined to become the Crossfield Bus Station was just a vacant plot.

On the other side of Broad Street buildings had been cleared to make way for what would eventually become Tiffany's Nightclub and the office block known as Crown House. These were jointly constructed at a cost of £250,000 and opened in 1968.

The land which later became the site for Halifax's ten pin bowling alley, around the corner of Orange Street near the Odeon, is still occupied by a variety of tightly-packed properties in this picture.

George Street was part way through the development which would be completed seven years later, it is clear from this picture that much work had barely begun on building the shops opposite Somerset House.

At Ward's End the Regal Cinema dominates the corner plot nearest to the camera; around the corner the Palace Cinema, built in 1905, and later replaced by a modern office building complete with a Wimpy Bar beneath it, is in view.

The photograph reveals just how much Market Street has changed over a period of around half a century; the Prince's Arcade, the Lower Market and the older property adjacent to them have been replaced by a supermarket and office buildings. Behind this area the abattoir is visible, a surprisingly large building when seen from above. North Bridge lies at the top left of the scene with the Grand Theatre to the right of it, and a busy Halifax railway goods yard beyond that.

Towards the bottom right of the picture, on the site now occupied by *The Halifax,* is Ramsden's Brewery. On the other side of Portland Place, the busy route which becomes Huddersfield Road, is the Electric Cinema which, in later years, found use as a snooker hall.

Good views along Southgate, Commercial Street and Market Street are afforded by this aerial photograph dating from1961.

The considerable size of the Borough Market and surrounding arcades is amply demonstrated here and its position in the centre of Halifax appears symbolic and insurmountable. By 1961 The Palace Theatre had been replaced by the new offices, shops and Wimpy Bar on this corner of Ward's End. The new buildings on George Street had been completed now and the Bus Station at Crossfield is fully operational. Note that the section of Broad Street alongside the bus station is, at this time, organised with one-way traffic. Beyond the bus station there is a small bus park next to Orange Street with about a dozen double deckers standing upon it. Further towards the top of the picture rows of terraced houses dominate the scene; the photograph is far to early to show the new inner relief road, or even the blocks of flats which now rise to the skyline here.

The appearance of Cow Green has changed radically since the time depicted here; gone is the Grand Junction Hotel and the properties next to it, to be replaced by a multi-storey car park and a greatly widened section of the road.

Opposite the Odeon Cinema, and down towards Northgate, land has been cleared which would eventually become the site for the bowling alley and, later, a large supermarket with roof-top car parking. On the subject of car parking, keen observers will notice that construction is underway on the multi-storey facility at Bull Green at the building where *Comet* was later to be situated. When this picture was taken there was a roundabout at Bull Green and Ward's End, but no traffic lights yet. The top left-hand corner of the picture is a mix of closely packed terraced houses and small industrial premises. The coming of the new relief road would cut a swathe through this area and change the character of this part of Halifax forever. The photograph shows a time before it became dominated by the out-of-town shopping parks which attract people from all over the district.

At the junction of Gibbet Street and Broad Street Ebenezer Church, complete with extended garden and paved area in front of it, is clearly in view. Interestingly, further along James's Road the large dark outline of the Alhambra can be discerned. There are few available images of this fine old building, particularly showing it near the end of its life, so this one is a particular treasure. The Alhambra, initially the Oddfellow's Hall, was built in 1840. It had the distinction of having Charles Dickens and Franz Liszt appearing at the venue. In common with many similar houses it was run as a cinema, opening as such in 1917 and showing films until 1959. It was demolished two years after this picture was taken, in 1963.

Traffic can be seen in considerable volume running along Southgate and Market Street in pre-pedestrianisation days.

Above: It were grim. There seems to have been little to smile about in this crowd scene from Thrum Hall. Perhaps the supporters were disappointed with the performance of their team.. or just mildly irritated by the photographer distracting them from the action on the field. Some of the headgear interesting to the modern eye; the size of the flat caps worn by some of the older fans shown here is almost comic. It is nice to see one or two ladies in the crowd of over 60 years ago. Halifax won two famous Wembley Rugby League Cup Finals in the 1930s. The first was in 1931 against York, seen by a Wembley crowd of 40,000, when Halifax won by 22 points to 8. The match is still considered to have been one of the best ever seen at Wembley. Towards the end of the decade Halifax were in the final again, this time against Salford, and the crowd of over 55,000, including about 8,000 Halifax fans, saw them beat the opposition with by a convincing 20 points to 3.

Right: There was Speedway at the Shay from 1949 when the police awarded a certificate entitling the Halifax Speedway Co. Ltd to admit up to 25,000 spectators to the venue. The first dirt track racing in an organised form took place at Thrum Hall, on the cricket ground, in 1928. Participants in the early races would often ride their machines to the track from their homes in neighbouring towns as well as Halifax. Ordinary road machines were used in those days, stripped of lights and non-essential parts, to be watched by up to 5000 spectators. The Dukes elephant mascot was derived from the success of the Duke of Wellington's Regiment in India in 1807. The regiment earned the right to use an elephant as their symbol because of "their good conduct and exemplary valour during the period of its service in India".

Wheels of time

Left: An unusual view of Commercial Street taken from this elevated position at the bottom side of George Square. The scene is dominated by the number 71 double-deck tram which, when the old man climbed aboard, would have travelled away from the position of the camera en-route to Highroadwell. George Gledhill, the gent's hosier and glover's premises on Commercial Street, seen here at the top of the picture, just to the right of centre. Coming towards the camera we see Cheapside and then the Prudential Assurance Offices, followed by the Westminster Bank. The motorcycle in the bottom corner of the picture may be a Velocette, judging by the characteristic 'fishtail' exhaust pipe. At the time this picture was taken there were approximately 500 motorcycles registered in the Borough of Halifax - and around 3,500 private cars. Tram statistics are harder to come by, but it is known that in 1903 there was a fleet of 93 trams operating in the town, a considerable investment in public transport at the time.

Above: The First World War saw a trial of this mobile catering unit on the tramways of Halifax. The vehicle was one of two 'Demi-cars' purchased by the Corporation in 1906 which fell out of favour with the operators and were withdrawn from service after an accident. *The Halifax National Kitchen,* as it was called, is featured here in 1916. Eagle eyes may just be able to make out the silhouette of the driver and two catering assistants, along with details of the menu which included soup and dumplings at 1d each, and ginger pudding for 2d. The mobile kitchen would follow a published route but spend much of its time positioned at Barum Top near Bull Green. It is said that it served up to 1000 meals per day before it was withdrawn in 1919.

Speaking in 1949 the Chief Constable of Halifax, Mr G. F Goodman said "Never in my 27 years police experience have I seen a street so congested with buses as Albion Street".

Below: The enterprising owner of the restored former Halifax double decker bus that can be seeen around Halifax at the time of writing should be applauded, and supported, for giving our 'nostalgia cells' a frequent top-up. In *our day,* of course, the buses were not always so well turned out; there was a distinctive aroma, especially on rainy days, of tobacco and seat fabric; this, combined with the the sound of whining gearboxes and chattering passengers, is indelibly etched in the minds of regular bus users from the time. This Halifax single decker operated by Hebble buses not only served the purpose of getting people from A to B, but it also helped to promote that great Halifax product, Webster's *perfect* ale.

The wheels of time section continues after the colour section of this book

> "...NEVER..HAVE I SEEN A STREET SO CONGESTED WITH BUSES AS ALBION STREET"

Nostalgia in colour!

Left: A familiar landmark on the industrial landscape of the town, Halifax Power Station generated electricity for 82 years until it closed in 1970. Adjoining the power station were two 170ft tall cooling towers, known affectionately by many as 'Salt and Pepper'. Attempts to demolish them with high explosives in March 1974 met with failure, to the huge disappointment of thousands of spectators who had turned out to witness the event. The 50 lb charge succeeded only in dropping one tower some 15 feet, leaving it poised at a dizzy angle on the concrete below. Both structures were eventually reduced to rubble by a demolition ball swinging from a tower crane. The power station itself was demolished during 1975 by Thomas Ward's of Sheffield at no cost to the Council in view of the high value of the scrap contained within the building. A sub-station for distributing power to the National Grid remained on the site.

Halifax was one of the first towns in the West Riding to be converted for north sea gas supplies. This was partly because the coal carbonising plant in Halifax was on its 'last legs', and a significant contributor to the unpleasant atmosphere in town.

Above: North Bridge in the distinctive *green* and cream paint work it enjoyed for many years. This photograph was taken in 1969, not long before the overhead road way would transform the area for ever and cause the demolition of the property seen on the left of the picture. If you say it quickly, *1969* doesn't sound like too long ago, yet a glimpse at the prices in the 'Courier from the time shows how much things have moved on. In that year a semi-detached house in fashionable Savile Park or Skircoat Green would have cost just £3,000; a two year old Triumph Herald was only £575, but you could have found a reliable second hand car for £150 upwards; Bottomley's Radio Cars were advertising all white luxury wedding cars from 'just £4 per wedding', and an oven-ready chicken cost less than eight *bob* (40p) at the Co-op.

Below: Liley's toy and pram store, had a popular position close to Commercial Street and supplied many Halifax households with the equipment they needed for looking after their offspring. Joseph Liley O.B.E was the managing director of the company and Mayor of Halifax between 1969 and 70. Joseph Liley was a Liberal councillor for Pellon at one time. He passed away in 1975 at the age of 70. Cheapside retailers have enjoyed a good passing trade for as long as most people can remember. It is an important thoroughfare through town linking Commercial Street and Southgate, with the added attraction of having one of the two side-entrances to Marks and Spencer's situated along it.

Above: A nostalgic view of the Woolshops area before it was developed, showing the location of several of the best-known traders in Halifax. Despite the obvious changes, the shape of the modern street remains distinctly similar.

The Union Cross, the oldest pub in Halifax is seen lower down the street, and, next to that is Van Allan, an outfitter with branches throughout the north and beyond. The Famous Army Stores stood on the corner of Old Market and Northgate and supplied camping equipment and outdoor clothes to the hardy people of Halifax for many decades.

Top: A delightfully nostalgic view of Market Street which is almost certain to rekindle memories of how Halifax used to be in the not-too-distant past. The scene is given an added

Above: Five traders dominate this photograph of Old Market, taken in 1969. Burtons the tailors had this building specially built in 1932. Virtually every town you can mention had a branch of the popular tailors, it became a major success story in British retailing. The Halifax branch had a snooker hall on the first floor. Next door, one of the town centre's historic buildings, occupied here by a favourite shoe shop, another national institution of its day, Freeman Hardy and Willis. The building was later purchased by the Halifax Courier and reopened as travel agents.

helping of nostalgia by the inclusion of the ubiquitous Ford Thames van, forerunner of the modern Ford Transit, and an essential element of thousands of small businesses for twenty years. The Prince's Arcade was built in 1931 and the parade of shops shown in this picture replaced a line of tatty old advertising hoardings which had stood here for several years. The Bon Bon coffee bar pictured here may bring back a memory or two; it always seemed inviting inside, with the fish net decorated with fairy-lights hanging from the ceiling and the noisy coffee machine making frothy drinks to go with the fresh ham sandwiches.

Left: A scene from 1973 along Northgate. The eye is drawn to the fascia sign on the Far East restaurant. The eating place was famous for several things, but the one we shall mention here is the good value lunchtime 'specials' which tempted office workers and business people to the restaurant, keeping it busy during the week. The modern-looking building on the left of the picture is the HQ of Timeform - the racing information business built up by the shrewd local entrepreneur Phil Bull.

Right: The bottom end of town, in the Church Lane area, with the floodlights of the Shay football ground in the background, and a number of elephants silently troop up the road towards the centre. The picture dates from 1972, and the elephants were performing the function of a 'live' advertisement for the circus which had come to town. There had been much controversy in Halifax, as in other British towns about the welfare of animals and whether the Council should allow Circus operators to perform with 'wild' animals on public land. There were many protests from animal welfare organisations, and their rows with circus proprietors were widely reported in the press and on television. Manor Heath was the venue for many enjoyable circus shows, often these were the only times children would get to see exotic animals 'in the flesh'. The sights, sounds, (and smells!) of the Big Top would create memories in local children which would stay with them forever.

Left: A view along Southgate dating from 1970, a year or two before the market buildings were stone cleaned, and depicting a time when traffic could flow relatively freely along the street. The picture is dominated by the fascia sign for 'The Salad Bowl', but signs for Wilbefort and Fred Moore's are visible further along. Southgate was once the most highly prized location in Halifax among retailers. Shops changed hands infrequently and any vacant property was quickly snapped up. The mid 1990s saw a decline in the popularity of this, once thriving location, and an air of panic eventually set in among those with an interest in the well-being of Halifax retailers. Attempts began to support local retailers. Out-of-town shopping parks and an increasing concentration of power in favour of the national retail organisations made trading conditions difficult for the long established local firms based in the town. Officialdom has now accepted its duty to support the traders who have helped to make Halifax what it is today. Let's hope that efforts designed to rescue the retail heart of Halifax will prevail in the uncertain times ahead.

Right: A picture of the tudor cottage in Shibden Park which was taken in October 1970. To the horror of many, it was demolished less than a year later.

Below: One of the best-known and respected names in ladies fashions in Halifax was Modelle's. Local women will remember how Modelle's used to be *the* place to go for that wedding outfit or the special dress for the works dance or posh dinner. Albert Birtle originally started the business in April 1927. It was located in Silver Street before moving to its more familiar position at the top of Woolshops. The business employed specialist fitters, a porter and a window dresser, and, in later years was overseen by the founder's daughter. The elegant store was well known for the quality of the designer clothing it offered, and could be relied upon to supply clothes which would get the wearer noticed for all the right reasons. The building occupied by Modelle's was very stylish and it is pleasing that the ones which replaced it

followed a similar design.

In this photograph, taken in May 1973, it comes as quite a surprise initially to see the Hillman saloon parked at the top of Woolshops and realise that traffic would come and go freely up and down the street in the days before it was 'pedestrianised'.

The half-timbered shop which caused its fair share of controversy in Halifax is featured on the left of the scene. The renovation of the building, thought to be one of the oldest in the district, was to cost the developers £250,000. It was later painted red and white as the boffins think that this was probably the original colour of the building. *Non-boffins* could be forgiven for thinking that building is more of a replica than the genuine article, and some may question the real value of renovating it to the extent to which it looks as if it were constructed last week!

Right: Another Charity Gala float, this time it is based on a Ford Thames Trader lorry sponsored by Smith's the popular Ford motor dealers. The vehicle, sporting the sign 'Queen of the Gala' is seen passing Greenwoods the gents outfitter which occupied this property at 25-27 Northgate for many years.

Above: The origins of Halifax's desire to build a ring road around the town can be traced back as far 1947. The need for a route to take traffic out of the centre and of the narrow bottlenecks around the centre had been apparent for many years. At various times the issue was called the 'biggest decision the Council would make in the history of Halifax'. In 1967 the Minister of Transport gave approval for the scheme, and in 1970 confirmation of a government grant for 75% of the cost of the massive undertaking was received. Perhaps the most remarkable aspect of the new road was the very short time it took to construct, despite a ten week strike by building workers; it was opened in April 1973, just two years after work began at a cost of £4.5 million. The opening was marked, among other things by a ' walkabout' involving around 20,000 local people on the newly-surfaced roadway.

The design of the Burdock way, named after Alderman Burdock a well-known servant of the town, is breathtaking in places. The span above Dean Clough and North Bridge is supported by huge concrete pillars which went on to win awards from ' The Concrete Society' for their design and construction. The project was planned on the basis that it would 'solve the traffic problems of Halifax' up until the year 2001.

1982 saw the work begin at last on the King Cross by-pass, a stretch of road which would complete the improved access to Lancashire and beyond.

Above right: An rather artistic view of Wainhouse Terrace with Wainhouse Tower, built by the creator of the unusual row of houses, in the distance. The square tower-like structure linked to the small houses by the arched bridge, contains a spiral staircase joining the upper and lower floors. Wainhouse's love of detail is demonstrated by the beautifully bevelled pillars and the ornamental slots fashioned in the square tower to give the impression of it being much older than it is.

There are only a few images of Wainhouse Tower in the book yet is surely the best known landmark in the town, standing 282 feet high and costing around £10,000 when it opened in 1875. John Wainhouse had commissioned the structure which was originally designed to act as a conventional mill chimney to take smoke away from his dye works in the Washer Lane area.

Left: Halifax Unitarian Church at Northgate End is featured in this photograph from 1982. The highly decorated place of worship could lay claim to a fascinating history. Daniel Defoe, author of *Robinson Crusoe* worshiped here when he visited Halifax. There had been churches on this spot for over 300 years and the building shown here dated from 1872. For some years this was the only church in Halifax apart from Halifax Parish Church. Halifax Orchestral Society was founded in the building, as was the first Scout troop in the area. The mid 1950s saw the congregation dwindle to the extent where it had to share a minister. In 1979 the church closed because the congregation had fallen to around a dozen regular members, and the building was sold for the sum of £13,000 to the Passenger Transport Executive. The property, along with the furniture store owned by F. S & B Clarke (Furnishings) Ltd. which had been damaged the same year in a serious fire, were pulled down in 1982. the site became part of the new Halifax bus station, and part of the former Sion Sunday School was carefully dismantled, restored and rebuilt a short distance from its original location.

Right: Cow Green as it appeared at the start of the 1960s. A congested traffic route which provided endless frustration for travellers at busy times of the day. All the property in this picture was pulled down in order to build the Cow Green multi-storey car park which now dominates this location. The car park was completed in 1971. Road improvements have included widening by one extra carriageway in each direction, the introduction of traffic lights (however did we manage without them?) and the construction of a sub-way at Cow Green to improve the safety of pedestrians crossing this busy route. The sub-way was pre-constructed and set in place in 1970. The *Evening Courier* carried reports of how difficult it was at the time to get people to use the sub-way in preference to dodging the traffic. Eventually railings were erected to make it difficult for people to cross above ground, and this seemed to do the trick.

The '1960s' feel to the scene is given weight by the delightful selection of motors in their rich colours depicted here. Duo-tone colour schemes were popular in those days, good examples can be seen on the Morris Oxford and Anglia van in the picture.

The name 'King Cross' is said by some to be derived from a visit to the area by King Canute - around *one thousand years* ago. Others think that a more likely origin of the name may be a stone cross standing in the area with some royal connection. A third theory suggests that it may be connected with a 'King' family which once 'provided' local officials to the townships of Warley and Skircoat, and may have been responsible for the erection of a guidestone marking the routes to Rochdale and the Calder Valley. Take your pick from this selection!

Above: The police station which stood on the junction of Burnley Road and Warley Road was established as such at around 1910. It was opened by Alderman L. Calvert,

chairman of the Halifax Watch Committee. At one time the station provided living accommodation for the single policeman who worked there, but this was abandoned in the 1950s.

This corner site has seen other uses over the last two centuries. An older property stood here before the police station. The building was formerly the Methodist New Connexion Chapel which opened in 1829. At the time it was described as the 'only dissenting place of worship in the village'. In 1876 church officials organised the construction of a new church in Leadenhall Street. The old building became the King Cross Working Men's Club, and later a furniture store for James Hoyle and Son, the King Cross removal firm.

King Cross used to be a village. When St. Paul's Church was built that side of the road leading to Queen's Road was lined with trees, three or four deep, right along the road. This picture was taken in November 1973.

Wheels of time continued

Above: A row of smartly presented double-deckers parked alongside the depot on Skircoat Road. They were unusual for two reasons; the pitched roof design and the open, curved rear staircase which was favoured by Halifax Corporation at the time. Tram lines were still very much in evidence in the 1930s when this picture was taken. Trams were eventually withdrawn from service in 1939, the last tram journey being from Mason Green in Illingworth to the tram depot in Skircoat Green.

Below: If buses still looked as cute as this perhaps more people would use them! The single-decker featured here was operated by Hebble from their depot at Ward's End on the site of the A.B.C cinema. It is good to see, at the time of writing, an elderly, but pristine double decker, in the old Halifax green and orange livery in daily service around the town.

Above: This is a pleasing sight for anyone interested in old motorcars, though the black and white print doesn't really do the vehicles justice. Of course, many of the motors in this picture would have been finished in *Henry Ford* style black livery, but a fair proportion of the others would be painted in deep maroons, rich navy blues and bottle greens which characterised the endearing vehicles of the 1930s and '40s. We were surprised to see that bunting was seen to be as much an aid to selling second hand cars as it is in some garage forecourts today.

"BY 1955 THERE WERE 7767 VEHICLES REGISTERED IN HALIFAX - TWICE AS MANY AS IN 1939"

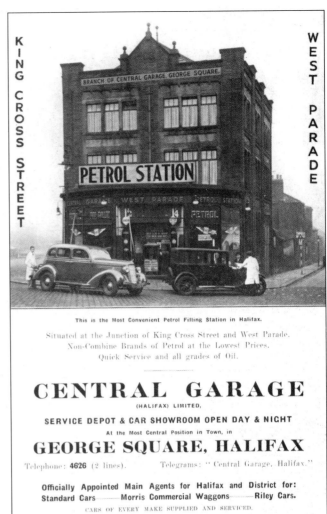

Above: A 1936 advertisement for Central Garage, the most centrally located showroom in town, according to its proprietors

Below: Carefully laid out cobble stones were a distinctive feature of the sweeping curve alongside Hoffman's car showroom on Huddersfield Road. Wilfred Pickles, the popular radio entertainer, is reputed to have returned to the well-known motoring establishment to buy his Rolls Royce motorcars from time to time. Pickles had close associations with Warley and transmitted the 250th edition of 'Have a Go' from there.

Below: A Whitaker's *of Halifax* delivery truck captured on camera, probably in the late 1950s. The Commer six-wheeler is making a delivery; note the open trap-door to the cellar of the establishment concerned, at the right of the truck. There was something almost patriotic, in a local sense, about Whitaker's slogan *Cock of the North;* it was a sad day for Halifax in 1968 when the Seedlings Mount Brewery at Corporation Street was taken over by Whitbreads. During the last two centuries more than a dozen local breweries have come and gone in the district. 'Gone' usually meaning their absorption into the larger national brewing concerns as the industry becomes concentrated in the hands of a small number of massive players. The most recent brewing loss to Halifax was Websters Fountain Head Brewery which had operated in Halifax since 1837. It is difficult to accept why hard working local people, making a product that customers obviously want to buy, should find themselves out of work as a consequence of these mergers, takeovers and big city deals; This applies to many industries these days and few people feel really secure in their jobs. This is one aspect of daily life that really was better, for most of us at least, in days gone by.

Above: By 1955 there were 7667 motor vehicle registered in Halifax - twice as many as there were in 1946, and 70% more than there were in 1939. A high proportion of the vehicles in this figure were motorcycles, 756 in all. The figures were produced by the motor vehicle taxation department of the Borough Council. In those days it was the local authority's job to collect the revenue from motor vehicle taxation. Records show that in 1955 a total of £134,000 was realised in Halifax.

A familiar sight on Halifax roads for a century - Joe Dean & Sons

The connection between Joe Dean and haulage goes back to the turn of the century. Joe Dean was the great grandfather of the present managing director and he rented several local farms from the Wheelwright family who were land and property owners.

Joe Dean

In 1919 the Wheelwright estates were sold off and Joe Dean bought Far Syke House, which is still the base of Joe Dean's business today. The haulage side of the business started in 1897. This involved delivering coal from the railway drops two miles away to the various mills in Greetland, using two horses and carts that had Joe Dean's name emblazoned on the side. Joe's son, Joe Willie, joined the business as a schoolboy, working part-time.

He would be sent with an empty horse and cart to the coal drops where he would get them loaded up and drive to the local mills where the boilerman would help him to unload. Even at weekends the carts were not idle; a waggonette body would be put on the back and was then used to take local people on day trips.

Joe Dean often bought his supply of horses from Appleby Horse Fair in Cumbria. Joe Willie and a drover would take their saddles with them and drive home fifty or sixty horses. This journey took three days.

The company branched out into longer distance haulage when a local mill, Binns & Sons, began to manufacture 'shoddy'; this is rags and waste wool pulled by machine and mixed back to a fibre. This was then mixed with a proportion of new wool and spun into yarn for blankets and heavy coating cloth. This involved collecting rags from Dewsbury and Morley and delivering the shoddy to Huddersfield. This work continued into the 1980s. The drivers would leave at 6am with 1s for Dewsbury and 1/6d for Morley, for expenses. With beer selling at that time for 2d, the stories of the horses bringing the drivers home at closing time and not the other way around are probably true. At that time a local dyeworks

Facing page, below: Joe Willie Dean is pictured fourth from the left in this 1920s photograph.

Left: A Morris Commercial lorry pictured at Brighouse Gala in 1934. The vehicle was supplied new by Service Garage, Brighouse and some of their staff are pictured.

Below left: A 1938 Leyland Cub BWX 138.

Below: Charabanc trips were an occasional feature of Joe Dean's business in the early part of the century. Lorries were converted to carry passengers for weekend trips to Hollingworth Lake and other local beauty spots.

were operating a very early Overtype Karrier, as were many other local mills, and this prompted Joe Willie to persuade his father to buy a similar motor lorry. This he did and the company went from strength to strength.

After the First World War two ex-War Department Albions were purchased at an auction sale in Halifax and were soon up and running, enabling the company to go on longer journeys. Also operating at this time was a Thorneycroft with a sided body, the rear half of which ipped for specialist use in the mill trade. The first two Leylands owned by the company were an RAF model and a 2¹/₂ tonner. Joe Willie particularly liked the RAF lorry because of its rugged construction but the 2 ¹/₂ tonner was remembered for more mundane reasons, Joe Willie was summoned for speeding in it through Eccles doing a staggering 16 mph!

During the 1920s and 1930s the work done by Joe Dean was mainly local, allied to the wool trade and the brick

and agricultural industries. The first garage was built in 1926, a tiny building which was only the width of the current roller shutter doors on the garage owned today.

Joe Dean died in 1931, leaving the business in the hands of his two sons, Joe Willie and Thomas Dean. The 1930s saw the firm's fleet updated with the purchase of two Leyland Cubs, both SKZ 3 models. One was bought in 1938 for £600 and was fitted with a Leyland cab and flat, dropsides were later added for £20. This vehicle was claimed by the War Department for only £320 when it was 15 months old. By the time that the Second World War broke out the company had a reasonably modern fleet, which was just as well, as there were no replacements available until 1949. *Cont overleaf*

Left: Basil Dean began his driving career in a cable-braked three ton Bedford. He went on to drive for 50 years and is pictured here in the 1960s.
Below left: An AEC lorry from the 1960s, which provided sterling service to Joe Dean.
Below: Three later AECs, this time Mercurys pictured in 1969.
Bottom right: One of the newest members of the fleet, a Foden flat backed lorry - a fast, technically advanced commercial vehicle that represents a huge progression from the fleet of years gone by.

From previous page. The 1940s saw the arrival of the third generation of Deans in the business, Joe Willie's sons, Basil and Ralph. Basil began his driving life behind the wheel of a Bedford at the age of 17 and he spent the next 50 years driving. The company never grew very big at that time, but the deliveries of firebricks to Sheffield provided a good income. The company kept their Leylands for reliability but began buying AECs in the late 1960s and they were soon the mainstay of the fleet.

The company suffered a tragedy in 1969 when Ralph died at the age of 39. As well as coping with the grief, this put extra work on the shoulders of the rest of the

family but in true Dean style the company pulled through what was a very difficult time, bringing in Basil's wife, Phyllis, to man the office.

During the 1960s and 70s the textile trade contracted and Joe Deans were soon carrying a variety of other goods; machine tools, plastics, fabricated steelwork and into the 1980s; chemical and engineering products.
In the early 1990s the fourth generation took over the reins in the form of Basil's son, Alan, and his wife, Diane. Now consisting of thirteen vehicles the make up of the fleet has altered dramatically. The company has two 38 tonne articulated lorries but the main demand is

for smaller rigid, multi-drop vehicles. The fifth generation has just joined the company. Alan's sons, James and Matthew are now working and training with the company.

Haulage is an ever changing business and with almost a century of history behind it, Joe Dean & Sons has seen more change than most. It is this ability for flexibility that will take the company through its centenary and well into the next millennium.

Down at the shops

George Street or George Square? many people are still confused over the correct name for one of the most famous streets in the town. George Square is the correct way to describe the area at the bottom of the incline, alongside Commercial Street and situated at the side of Lloyds Bank. Few people will be aware that this part of Halifax was originally known as Loveledge Lane, it was renamed after the King of Denmark who stayed for a night at Somerset House in 1768. The 19 year-old King was Christian VII, but he travelled as 'Prince George' in order to test the patience of future nostalgia book authors.

To the modern shopper George Street may seem as much a part of 'traditional' Halifax as any other familiar part of the town. The truth is though, that George Street has undergone tremendous changes in the last half century, changes which attracted controversy and endured delays in their execution. The street, in the 1930s was narrow and congested, with a single tram line serving the Highroad Well route running along it. The tramline had been laid here in 1912. Proposals to widen the street were made as far back as 1912, a reflection of the growing popularity of the area and the businesses located there. The changes which affected the area mainly concerned the right hand side of the street as we look up it. On the other side, Somerset House (1766) and Lloyds Bank (1898) have remained largely the same over the years, as has Imperial Chambers, located near the taxi rank at the bottom of the street, which was built in 1908 by George Webster &

Sons, tea blenders and coffee roasters.

The 1930s saw initial road widening and the start of the improvements which resulted in the layout of the street we recognise today. At the top of the street the Bull's Head public house was built to replace an establishment of the same name. The first Bull's Head had stood on the spot for at least two centuries and was the place where Halifax's Masonic Lodge of Probity was founded in 1738. The old Bull's Head closed in August 1940. Other commercial premises operating in the area at the time included Feavers the tobacconists, J.E Jowett's piano showroom, A. Cooke's the newsagent, H.K Woodward the chemist and J.H. Walton the fish and game supplier. At one time the offices of the *Halifax Guardian* were located here; in later years they were used by the Halifax Printing Works.

Initially the demolition of the older property and the building of the new shops and public house in 1940 resulted in only a marginal widening of the road. Over the years car parking spaces were added to the side of the road near the new buildings and changes were made to the proportion of the paved area versus flower beds on this side. Pictures, mainly postcards, dating from the 1950s onwards show that the new seats in this oasis for shoppers were very well used by people eager to take a break from their bargain hunting, and admire the neat flower beds.

The one-way traffic system we know today was introduced to George Street in September 1963, at the same that one-way traffic became the norm along Rawson Street.

Above: The clarity of this picture belies the fact that it is over 100 years old. The scene was captured in central Sowerby Bridge , the road in the picture being Town Hall Street. the cobbled road contains clear evidence of the main form of transport through the town - horses! The scene dates from a time before trams were introduced. Trams initially ran on the route from Halifax from 1902, the route was later extended to Ripponden. The building on the left became the home of Barclays Bank. The dour clothing and the lovely street lamps add atmosphere to the scene.

Below: A rare view of Gibbet Street as it was more than sixty years ago. Superficially it really hasn't changed all that much at the time of writing. Victoria Fisheries, owned for many years by Albert Sunderland, may no longer exist, but the chemist's business trading under the name of Frank Swire is still there at the junction of Gibbet Street and Queen's Road. At one time this was the main route that trams would have taken to Highroadwell from the centre of Halifax. They would clatter up and down this busy route from early morning until late at night.

Below: Union Street, once the heart of the town's commercial activities, pictured on a wet day in the 1930s. It is thought that the street took its name at the time of the Jacobites, a time when the word 'union' was as popular as the word 'national' is today. The administrative buildings of Halifax were once located in this area before the present town hall was built, and this led to the naming of a public house - the Town Hall Tavern - which stood on Union Street for decades. Up until the 1950s the area was notorious for the traffic jams caused largely by buses and before them, trams. The situation was eased by moving several of the busiest stops to different streets in the town. Local folk will immediately think of Pearson's Fish Buffet and Henley's Herbal stores when they recall memories of Union Street. The outline of tramlines can just be made out. At the top left of the picture the highly decorated tram standard is in view; its purpose was to carry the current for the vehicles, with a secondary use, as seen in the picture, of providing a place from which to hang an electric street lamp. The Lower Market, which closed at the end of 1968, is just in view in the distance. The bottom part of the Lower Market used to be used as a British Restaurant during the Second World War. British Restaurants were part of a national scheme intended to provide a supply of wholesome food at reasonable prices and act as an element in a wider contingency in case of disruption to public services.

The Lower Market (almost always referred to as the *Low* Market) was a place with much to offer; spicy aromas would greet you on entering either of the two doors, and children would be seen staring at the 'unusual' foodstuffs which could be found there, such as tripe, elder, a massive variety of pickled goods and last, but not least, black puddings. An impressive range of other products was on offer too, from biscuits to paperback books, and from linoleum and its colourful salesmen to Christmas decorations and household china.

Right: King Cross has been the subject of much attention over the years. An area of tightly-knit, in every sense of the word, housing, much of which had outdated facilities and was in poor condition. Dampness, bulging walls, leaning chimneys, and outside lavatories had characterised the area for many years. The blocks of outside toilets were up to 50 yds away from a family's home and attracted petty thieves and vandals who would steal the fittings and damage the workings. Of course, there were exceptions to this grim list, and some householders were so determined to remain in their homes when clearance plans were announced that they appealed against the demolition order.

February 1968 saw many of the homes succumb to the demolition contractors. A two-acre site containing around 200 properties was cleared by contractors working for the Council in order to make way for the construction of the town's new fire station. Some of the names swept away forever included Dublin Street, Cork Street, Nile Street, St. Paul's Street, Mary Street, Walton Street, Swaine's Terrace, Garside Street and Spring Street. Most of the houses were around 100 years old by the time they reached their undignified end, falling into dusty heaps with hitherto private, wallpapered interiors exposed by the mechanical onslaught. Francis Fascione and his demolition experts from Elland played a leading role in the clearance of King Cross, and the transformation of a community of 200 dwellings into a pile of rubble weighing 10,000 tons.

The Old King, standing across the way from the old police station and alongside the route towards the Calder Valley and Sowerby Bridge was demolished in February 1975. At the same time, 59 houses met the same fate in a scheme which had been in the pipeline for at least 12 years.

Left: Around fifty members of staff from Marks and Spencer's pose for the obligatory photograph before setting off on a day trip to York. The fashions of the day as shown here, are certain to bring back memories; wide collars, exaggerated cuffs and huge buttons, not to mention the popular pearl necklaces and brooches worn by almost every smart lady of the day. It would have been a poor carry on if you couldn't have been *fashionable* when working at the town's leading clothing shop!

The ladies are pictured in front of *Jackson's,* 'the complete home furnishers for complete satisfaction' according to the sign in their window. The popular retailer of T.Vs, pianos and home furnishings was situated along Cornmarket, next door to F. Priestley the ladies hairdresser and Stead and Simpson's.

Below: Immediately before the redevelopment of the Woolshops area this part of Halifax was in serious decline. The importance of this section of the town, over a period of two centuries or more, was assured by the fact that it was a main route into Halifax for travellers approaching from the east. These travellers, among others, would have been concerned with selling wool to independent weavers in the shop and warehouse properties which were gathered here, leading quite naturally, to the area becoming known as 'Woolshops'. It is said that Halifax is the only town in the country to have street with this name.

poor-quality property, including housing, from the core of each typical northern town, and to relieve the congestion which was gradually bringing the town centre to a standstill. Throughout the north, this was the age of the 'ring road', concrete and car parks, high rise flats and bingo halls.

In terms of her one-stop shopping centre Halifax was something of a late developer in comparison to neighbouring towns. Plans had been put forward as far back as 1951 for a centralised shopping area. In common with other towns, the objective was to create a 'showpiece shopping centre' for Halifax. The benefit of hindsight suggests that a

The 1960s and 70s saw tremendous activity throughout Britain by property developers eager to create modern new shopping centres in the heart of virtually every town large enough to support one. In the years immediately after the end of the war most of their attention had been directed towards London, where the rebuilding of the Capital offered lucrative contracts and a near insatiable demand for office accommodation, shops and housing. In the '60s the attention of the large building concerns turned to the regions, the north of England being particularly well represented. Government restrictions relating to civil construction work meant that local authorities had to form partnerships with major builders in order to carry out retail developments. This was the most dynamic period in the recent history of town centre architecture. Neighbouring Bradford broke new ground with the construction of the Arndale Centre, followed soon after by smaller towns such as Burnley. The motivation was not just a desire to 'keep up the Jones's' by local planners and councillors; there was a real need to clear

more pressing reason was the need to 'keep pace' with developments in other towns, and to make sure that the major retailers of the day would be attracted to our town on equal terms.

There was as you would expect, considerable controversy surrounding the issue and most of it related to the scale of the undertaking and the extent to which existing buildings, businesses and facilities would be affected. In the 1970s, the project was referred to as the Arndale scheme (aren't we lucky the name didn't stick?) and plans for a much larger centre than the one we know today were contemplated. Looking back at the records it appears that the Arndale centre would have been similar in appearance to the ones built in towns adjacent to Halifax, in as much as they would have been of the 'undercover' variety. Estimated costs had been calculated to be as high as £30 million for the most lavish proposal in the late 1970s. The Civic Trust became involved and a public inquiry considered the merits of the large versus the more modest scheme. The outcome

was that the smaller option was chosen in preference to the covered scheme. The scale can be appreciated when one considers that the final centre cost a relatively modest £6.5 million.

Further controversy surrounded the future of Halifax's oldest timbered building situated at the top of Woolshops. It was historic, without question, but it was also in poor condition. The outcome was that the cost of renovating the building, a sizeable £250,000, was met by the developers and the property was saved. After many delays and a considerable amount of contemplation, the final plan was agreed, developers appointed and work began. The construction work was completed in 18 months and the new facility was opened in October 1983 by the managing director of Boots, one of the major participating stores in the development. The businessman in question was Keith Ackroyd, the Halifax-born retailing supremo and former pupil of Heath Grammar School.

Above: It is surprising how quickly time marches on. This picture only dates from 1968, but the changes on Northgate since this time have been dramatic. Obviously, the buildings on the right of the photograph made way for the construction of the new central library and council offices, the biggest development to affect Northgate in the history of the area. The top of Gaol Lane, a narrow passage with much history associated with it can be seen next to Gibson Dixon's premises on the right of the picture. Gaol Lane is known now as the location of Halifax's main Post Office; at one time there were five pubs down that street and it was not advisable for the unwary to venture down it at certain times of the day! *British Relay,* the television rental company, is the shop on the other side of Gaol Lane. Further along Northgate, and right in the background of this photograph, was Willis's. Their sign outside proclaimed "bargains are our business - and you save". Most of us can remember a trip to their clothing department store; they were renown for good value and a wide choice of garments. They used a system of overhead vacuum tubes to carry money and messages from the cash tills, as many of the busier, traditional stores did in days gone by. Santa's Grotto at Willis's was another popular attraction in the weeks leading to Christmas. It was a sad day for Halifax when their doors closed for the last time.

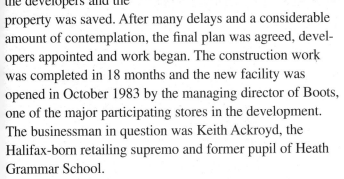

Left: A deserted Woolshops in a picture from 1968. The gentle curve of Beacon Hill is in the background and the clock tower of the Parish Church standing as it has for over 500 years, can be seen below it. The New Talbot public house was situated near the street lamp in this picture, below the Prince's Arcade.

Robertshaws, purveyors of all things electrical since 1934

Harold Robertshaw was born in Mytholmroyd in 1899, the son of a weaver. He began his working life at the tender age of twelve, working as a half-timer learning to weave in a local mill. His father taught him early on in his life that any man who knew how to weave would never starve, which was a very sound philosophy in those hectic days of numerous mills screaming out for experienced workers.

It was a long day for a young boy. Harold began his trek to work at 6am and his teeth would chatter mercilessly against the biting winter winds, as he walked behind his dad for shelter. Throughout this, Harold still went to school in the afternoon and night school in the evening. He changed careers soon afterwards, moving from textiles to sheet metal work for Stansfields of Hebden Bridge. He worked there for several years, except for a break when he served in the motor transport section of the Royal Army Service Corps during the First World War.

Harold was a pioneer in the radio industry, building his first wireless set in 1922. He and his brother opened a shop in Mytholmroyd, repairing wirelesses and selling records for gramophones.

He moved to Elland in 1934 and bought Arthur Greenwood's music shop in Southgate. His business remained along the same lines, selling and repairing radios, electrical goods and records.

His first week's takings amounted to just £5 but before long his experience shone through and the company grew, expanding eventually to sell and repair cycles. In those early days, Harold would repair the item and return it lovingly to its owner by horse and cart. He became a familiar sight around the streets and lanes of Elland in the 1930s.

In 1954 Harold's son, Adrian joined the company followed by his younger son, Julian in 1962. The company is still family owned with the third generation, Tony and Chris, joining the company in the 1980s.

The business has always remained in the same premises although it did expand to encompass the living area in 1966, for storage and showroom

Besides this, the company offers free local delivery and installation on all major appliances, which makes them very competitive.

The early philosophy taught to Harold by his father still rings true today, although the trade has changed. These days electronics is the one industry which is sure to grow and grow and anybody who knows anything about it is certain to succeed. The company also supports and sponsors local events and charities, ensuring the continuance of their good name in the community. In these days of fast technological advancement, Robertshaws are determined to help with a smooth transition into all new areas, including the new digital age, for customers old and new.

purposes. At this time the demand for more electrical appliances began to take precedence over the cycle and toy business and Robertshaws slowly phased this line out, concentrating their efforts on the more demanding side.

The company has built up a reputation of quality and is a specialist in electrical and domestic appliances. Selling up-to-the-minute equipment, the company also offers a complete back-up service for the goods they supply.

Investing in the local community has paid off. Providing the local public with a friendly and comprehensive service has meant that Robertshaws has a place in the hearts of Elland people. Customers return time and time again for their equipment; some who have moved out of the area still return!

Nowadays the company is a member of an international buying group called Euronics, which enables it to price match with major retailers or multiples, whilst still providing an excellent service.

Above: The founder, Harold Robertshaw at the London Olympia Trade Show in the 1930s. *Facing page, bottom left:* Robertshaws shop in the late 1930s, showing the division between the audio side and the cycle side of the business. *Centre:* Southgate, Elland from just after the turn of the century. The shop on the far right of the picture is now owned by Robertshaws. *Below:* Robertshaws shop as it is today.

Crossley Heath School - a story of progress and proud heritage

When, in the early 19th century, John Crossley, a hand weaver, bought Dean Clough, a small mill in Halifax, his wife, Martha declared, 'If the Lord does bless us at this place, the poor shall taste of it.' John died in 1837, but Martha lived to see her sons rich, their firm at the forefront of the world's carpet industry.

From the first, brothers, John, Joseph and Francis, put aside 10% of their mill profits for philanthropic purposes. This meant large gifts to the town, not the least being Crossley's orphanage.

The school was completed in 1864 and opened with the arrival of six little boys and their mothers. Girls were admitted the following year. The Deed of Foundation, establishing the school was only put into operation after John Crossley died. in 1870. 15 governors were chosen, 3 by the Town Corporation and 12 by certain independent churches.

Little is known of Mr Thomas Porter, a yarn merchant who donated £50,000 in 1887 on condition that his name was added to the charity. This was done by Royal Charter, and the school's financial difficulties, felt since 1882, were eased.

In the first 25 years, 1,100 children were admitted. They enjoyed a broader curriculum than children at local elementary schools, although, for girls, education was secondary to practical crafts and social training. The

school's 3rd headmaster, Mr. Barber began a new educational era. Examinations and results were the order of the day and the stick was seldom idle.. Despite the rigours of the regime, the children were essentially happy, with an affection for and loyalty to the school. An old boy of Mr. Barber's era has described the going-to-bed procedure. When 'one was called, boys knelt for prayers. At 'two', little wire baskets were placed on their beds. 'Three' mean folding coats neatly inside. By 'eleven' baskets were full

and placed as in the picture.
Boys waited patiently for 'twelve', that finally allowed them to climb into bed.
Until 1877, the school was under a single principal and, although not co-educational, some classes were mixed and the boys and girls mingled on social occasions and in the playground. In 1877, two departments were established under a separate headmaster and headmistress.

The Great War brought temporary changes and educational reform. The orphanage became a secondary school and open to fee-paying day scholars. A flourishing Old Scholars' Association helped to clear the school debts and provide a scholarship and the playing fields at Broomfield.

The school continued to expand and flourish until the Second War brought great changes. The boarding side was closed. The 1944 Education Act brought controversy until the future status of the school was settled in 1945. The school became voluntary controlled, maintained by the local Authority. Since then it has remained a selective grammar, becoming fully co-educational under a single head in 1968.

school houses, Kings and Queens. During the 19th century, parents, and eventually the government, demanded changes in the way the school operated and a new, much larger school was opened in 1879. More innovations over the years launched the school into the 20th century. Its reputation, deservedly, was sound, but the need for financial security persuaded the governors, in 1926, to pass the trusteeship of the school to the Halifax County Borough Council. Following the 1944 Education Act, the Crossley Heath School became a state grammar school for boys.

The Crossley Heath School
In 1985, Heath Grammar School and the Crossley and Porter School amalgamated to become a mixed grammar school, concentrated in the building of the C&P school. In April 1991, the Crossley Heath School became grant-maintained, once again outside local authority control.

Above: The Heath 1956/7 rugby 1st XV. **Main picture:** *This delightful photograph dates from 1866 when the school took in orphan children from the surrounding areas. Mr. Oliver and Mrs. Smith can be seen here with their pupils outside the main entrance.* **Facing page:** *The girls' dormitory dating from the early 1900s.* **Below:** *Crossley and Porter School Prefects, 1969.*

Heath Grammar School
'The Free Grammar School of Queen Elizabeth in the Parish of Halifax' was authorised by a Royal Charter, granted in February 1585. The first land, including the site at Heath, was given to the charity by Henry Farrar, Esquire in 1597. The Vicar of Halifax at that time successfully encouraged his parishioners to be more generous and was rewarded by being known as the school's founder. By 1727 the charity had become neglected and another charter, this time from King George II re-established it. Thus the school had two Royal Charters, reflected in the names of the two

Sowerby Bridge family firm goes from humble start to great future

This Sowerby Bridge firm of engineers merchants and mill furnishers had small beginnings -in a wash kitchen at Mill Bank. Ronald Sutcliffe left

school at 14 and, after a short spell as a doffer in the local mill, became apprenticed to Thomas Smith, an ironmonger in Halifax. On completing the apprenticeship, Mr. Sutcliffe obtained work with John Hall Ltd. and served at their Birmingham and Cardiff branches until the intervention of the Second World War.

Serving with the Royal Electrical and Mechanical Engineers Regiment, he rose to the rank of Staff Sergeant before his demobilisation in 1946. Until 1951, he went back to work for another local ironmonger before deciding to start his own business from home.

The dining table was his office and a cupboard under the stairs was his storeroom. His wife, Marjorie, who was

the village post mistress at the time, took orders over the phone which were then collected, booked out and delivered by Ronald.

When the cupboard overflowed, the stores were moved next door to a small wash kitchen. Soon, this too became too small and Mrs. Sutcliffe was demanding the return of her dining room table. The time had come to move along the road to the two-storeyed premises of a retired piano tuner. An assistant was set on and the paperwork was placed with local accountants.

Soon afterwards, the firm's present premises was purchased from Firths' Bakery. There was by this time a staff of four and Mr. Sutcliffe had become desk-bound.

In 1976, owing to Mr. Sutcliffe's sudden illness, the business was taken over by his daughter, Mrs. Christine Walker. She had obviously learned the trade well. Business flourished to the extent that it became necessary in 1979 to enlarge the offices. By now the company had a wide range of their requirements to offer to engineers' merchants and mill furnishers. Cutting tools included drills, reamers slot drills and holesaws. Safety products were in demand and Sutcliffes supplied welding helmets, face screens, ear-defenders and much more. Hand tools included goods from such manufacturers as Record, Ridgeway, Marples, Stanley and Bedford. Welding equipment and precision tools were on offer from leading manufacturers and, one of Sutcliffe's specialities, industrial fasteners of all types.

Above: Mill Bank, where it all began. **Right:** *The opening of the new offices in July 1979. Ronald Sutcliffe can be seen seated behind the desk.*

In 1981, as part of a plan for further expansion, a representative was appointed for the Brighouse and Elland areas. By now, the work force was 14 strong and the merchandise ranged from small hand tools to large industrial power tools. The company delivered daily to the areas surrounding their warehouse and the counter service for callers still flourished. Most items could be delivered immediately from the wide range of stock and other, more unusual items were obtained within two or three days. The firm's qualified staff were generous with their advice to customers. The welding side of the business was also increased.

At the time of the move to Firths' Bakery, Sutcliffes' stock had barely filled one room. By the time a computerised system was installed in 1984, it had to be loaded with 14,500 products.

Because of the high concentration of mills in the area and the other diverse industries near at hand, the firm's catchment area in the old days had been confined within a radius of ten miles from Sowerby Bridge. The firm had dealt only with trade but the recession of the late eighties took its toll of the local industry. The closure of local hardware and ironmongery businesses brought the general public to R. & M. Sutcliffe's door. They knew they could be sure of expert advice and

good quality goods. A new trade counter and display area were set up to encourage the cash customers in 1991, proving an immediate success.

No doubt, as local business picks up, after the nineties' recession, it will depend on the continued good services of R. & M. Sutcliffe Ltd.

Above: A view of Sowerby Bridge, home of R & M Sutcliffe since 1951. Below: R. & M. Sutcliffe, seen here before the white wall on the left was painted with the new company logo in 1990.

Outskirts

Right: This atmospheric scene dates from 1938 and gives a clear impression of what West Street, Sowerby Bridge was like at the time. The general layout of the area has changed little over the last sixty years in comparison to some other places featured in this book. The centre of the view is dominated by the Royal Hotel, a building which remains on this spot at the time of writing. There are elements in the scene which give

the era away, such as the tramline to Ripponden and the delightful gas lamps. The poster on the right of the picture advertises John West salmon with a slogan surprisingly similar to the one used today "Insist on the best and buy John West middle cut".

To the right of the poster is a hairdressers' lock up shop, with an advertisement for 'permanent waves'. There was a time when hairdressing establishments had individual booths within them where the ladies would have their hair permed, cut and coloured in private. Such was their desire for absolute secrecy in the salon. Another sign of the times can be found next door to the hairdressers' featured

here. It is a lock-up property with a sign in the window proclaiming it to be 'The King of the Tripe Dressers'.

Small er picture: The church on the left of this picture was founded by Weslyan Reformers on this site as far back as 1852. Before that Methodists had met in a house on Back Wharf Street, and later in a room at the Bull's Head Hotel. Tuel Lane Methodists Church as seen in this picture, was rebuilt here in 1874 at a cost of £3,000. It was extended in 1889 for a further investment of £2,000, which included the cost of a new organ.

Over the years the Church has faced many challenges; extensive dry rot in the late 1940s caused a terrific drain on the church's resources when the bill for the work amounted to £4000. There had been talk of a merger with the Bolton Brow Methodists for many years and this finally happened in 1978. There were practical reasons for this; a 450 capacity at Tuel Lane and 850 capacity at Bolton Brow was far in excess of the capacity needed to accommodate modern-day congregations, and the cost of the upkeep of these spacious properties was overwhelming.

Sadly a serious fire in later years was to gut the building on Tuel Lane which had been so carefully preserved over a period of 100 years. Local worshippers were not to be beaten, and in true 'Sowerby Bridge' fashion a modern place of worship was built on the site.

Above: In this photograph featuring a view down Keighley Road, past the junction of Shay Lane on the left, and on to Ovenden Road, we can see the Ovenden Cross public house on the right of the picture. The carefully arranged pattern of the cobbles is easily discerned; it is quite amazing to contemplate the massive amount of labour involved in quarrying, dressing and laying them, in their *millions.* The roadway had to be very durable, for this was a much-used route in and out of Halifax, both by travellers on their way to Bradford and by workers from Illingworth and Ovenden who laboured in the mills and factories in the centre of Halifax. Much of the shop premises and private housing on the right of the picture was later cleared to make way for small, new developments.

Top: This view of Holmfield is intriguing for a number of reasons, not least of which being the mysterious outline in the fields at the top right of the picture. At first sight this seems to be the preliminary work for a small housing estate, but the reality is that this was once the location of a temporary army camp, set up on this swampy ground in wartime Halifax. Initially the camp served as a convalescent depot, and after the war it became the home of a section of the Pay Corps. The camp was disbanded in the 1950s, and some people may remember the column of tanks which slowly made its way towards Keighley Road as the soldiers and their equipment pulled out of town.

Top: A view along Southgate, Elland which is thought to date from the 1940s. This scene had changed little on this narrow commercial stretch of the centre of Elland over a period of many decades. In later years it was the subject of much controversy as plans for the development of Southgate came and went.

Above: The Parish Church in Elland dominates this picture, a favourite composition of scores of photographers over many years. The parade of shops which includes Manchester House has a branch of Lloyds Bank on the right hand side. There had been a bank on this spot since 1894; Lloyds had been here since 1894. Manchester House and the adjacent shops had been trading here for many years, though the buildings themselves have been extensively modified.

Above: A rainy day in West Vale in a picture dating from the 1930s. The tram featured here is the enclosed type, earlier versions were open to the elements. The photograph evokes very nostalgic feelings, perhaps the combination of the tram, the damp cobbles and the old gas lamp are the cause. Trams on this route had to contend with the exceptionally steep gradient at Salterhebble. There was once talk of constructing a special 'tram lift' on that section of the route because of fears about the trams ability to climb and descend the steep gradient safely. Conditions around the Halifax area were less than ideal for trams because of the narrow streets as well as the hills and valleys.

Below: Whiteley's Corner, named after the long established newsagents and tobacconists featured here which later became involved in the retail travel business. The shop stood on the corner of Bethel Street. This picture dates from 1957. Barclays Bank can be seen on the right of the picture and the Pentecostal Hall and Albion Restaurant can be seen further along the same side of the road. the Morris half-ton van approaching the picture is of the type favoured by the Post Office for many years. Vehicles of this era always seem to have more personality than their modern equivalents - reminiscent, in some ways, of British black and white films from the 1950s.

Right: Sandwiched between Rochdale Road and Burnley Road, Wainhouse Terrace is one of several examples of the unusual building style adopted by J.E Wainhouse the mastermind behind thew construction of Wainhouse Tower. Wainhouse was well-known for embellishing ordinary buildings such as cottages with fine porches and ornate chimneys. The property at Wainhouse Terrace had many interesting features. Two bridges on the upper floor led to spiral staircases which joined it to the lower level, on which a row of single-storey dwellings was located. Cloisters added to the unusual design of this lower floor.

Left: Barely recognisable to the modern eye, this picture shows the usually busy junction on Burnley Road, King Cross. Here, Warley Road veers off to the right, Rochdale Road takes traffic down to Sowerby Bridge on the left, and travellers to the Calder Valley and beyond head on straight forward, past the row of dark, terraced houses which sit tight on the valley side beneath a mass of chimneys. The scene is given character by the beautiful victorian gas lamp, with outstretched 'arm' upon which the lamp-lighter would rest his ladder before scampering up it to light the flame. The area has changed much in the eighty-some years since the scene was recorded. Gone are the slippery stone setts, and the Police Station which once proudly guarded this route and the adjacent residents.

Copyright Lilywhite, Sowerby Bridge.

King Cross, Halifax. 32

Above: A nostalgic view of Cote Hill if ever there was one. In the centre of the picture a coal merchant is delivering coal - by horse and cart. With the aid of a magnifying glass the name of the merchant is revealed: 'Henry Crowther, Coal Merchant, St. Paul's Station'. He is listed in a 1936 directory of Halifax as having another depot at Battinson Road. The Ramsden's Brewery sign just past the horse and cart indicates the location of the Rose and Crown. The pub was closed during the last war and pulled down a few years afterwards. St. John's Church is on the right of the picture. The church was consecrated in September 1878 and it incorporates a Sunday School which was used as a primary school for local children between 1873 and 1926. Modern old-people's flats now occupy most of the area on the right of the picture and many of the old buildings in this scene have been cleared.

Left: This picture dates from the early 1930s and shows a busy shopping scene at King Cross. Notable features include the elegant tram standards which carried the electric current for the tramcars, the presence of stone cobbles, and the Old King public house which can be seen in the background.

Above: Mytholmroyd, some years after the end of the First World War. Hard-wearing cobble stones were the order of the day for this main road linking Yorkshire and Lancashire. Trams rattled and whirred up and down the Calder Valley on this route for over thirty years. The distance from the main power station in Halifax meant that 'booster stations' were needed to maintain an adequate current to drive the trams. There was one at Brearley, with its own generator. Just to the right of centre in this view the gable end of the Dusty Miller can be seen.

Top: Some readers may just be able to remember the transport company, Walton and Helliwell which used to be based at White Lee Mytholmroyd. Note their telephone number 'Telephone Mytholmroyd '49'. This photograph dates from the 1940s, note the *Power Petrol* advertising sign on the right of the picture. Also visible are the tramlines which formed the basis of the Calder Valley's main road-based public transport link with Halifax in the first quarter of the century. Unlike the rest of the district the long and relatively level run from Halifax to Hebden Bridge was well suited to trams, but this was not enough to prevent them from being superseded by 'buses in 1939.
In later years a Volkswagen car dealership operated from this spot. White Lee Garage later went on to offer second hand cars of any make when VWs ceased to be sold here.

Above: A view looking into the centre of Mytholmroyd, with the steep side of the valley leading up to Midgley providing a dramatic backdrop. Mytholmroyd's distinctive wide valley floor, though subject to serious flooding until the river Calder was eventually tamed, was suitable for modern industrial and residential development, being well connected by excellent road and rail links between Yorkshire and Lancashire. The most famous 'son' of Mytholmroyd is the Poet Laureate Ted Hughes. Born the son of a carpenter in the village, he left the area at the age of seven, but returned to live in the district in later life. Ted Hughes attended the local Burnley Road School as a youngster.
The road to Cragg Vale was the last road in the district to be 'turnpiked', and the last to have the toll system removed from it. The best known church in the area is Mytholmroyd's *St.Michael's,* built in 1848 at a cost of about £2,000. It was enlarged forty years later.

Above: A marvellous scene dating from 1922, depicting the unveiling of the War Memorial in Mytholmroyd, before of a crowd of well over 1,000 people. Modern visitors to the the community's War Memorial, featuring the unknown soldier and surrounding memorial gardens, find that it is one of the most attractively designed monuments of its kind in the district. It lies alongside the busy Burnley Road linking Yorkshire with Lancashire long before the M62 was ever thought of. This photograph was taken from the bridge across the River Calder. The bridge itself is ancient in origin, and parts of the stone structure date back to 1663. The building across the way is Calder Grange, a substantial early victorian house which became a young ladies' seminary from the 1860s, attracting pupils from all over Yorkshire. It was demolished in the 1960s.

Left: Anyone familiar with Mytholmroyd will instantly recognise this photograph of the railway bridge which caries the trans-Pennine railway line through the town. This almost deserted scene is not typical of the road which ultimately takes travellers up towards Cragg Vale and eventually, beyond that to Littleborough, Rochdale and the rest of Lancashire. The railway brought with it employment for many, not only because of the increased trading opportunities and ease of travelling to work, but also for those involved with the construction of the substantial bridges, viaducts, stations and miles of track.

Above: The Women's Voluntary Service, later to become the Women's Royal Voluntary Service, played an important role in attempts to support the war effort on the home front. Fifty - seven nations took part in the second war and Britain and the Commonwealth participated from the start to the finish. By the time war was declared on September 3rd 1939 preparations were in place; the evacuation of children began immediately with a staggering 1.5 million youngsters being sent away from likely targets immediately. By 1940, when the feared bombing had failed to materialise, the children were returned to their homes. Gas masks were issued to every man, woman and child - including babies, and people were required to carry them everywhere. There was, however, no gas attack on British soil during the war.

> ## "...THERE WAS, HOWEVER, NO GAS ATTACK ON BRITISH SOIL DURING THE WAR."

The WVS was not the only voluntary service with an important role to play in wartime; In May 1940 the Local Defence Volunteers was formed, later to become known as *The Home Guard*. In the first 3 days over 800 Halifax men signed up for the new organisation, tasked with providing a fall back position in the event of an invasion. Local appeals were made for Auxiliary Fire and Ambulance Personnel, along with Air Raid Wardens, resulting in a further 1500 volunteers coming forward.

Below: Remarkably, the appearance of this shop property, with upstairs living accommodation, has changed little in almost a century. The five businesses shown here have been a substantial part of Mytholmroyd's retailing community and have housed dozens of different types of shops during their time here beside the busy main road through the village. Mytholmroyd is a community steeped in history; the turnpike road dates from 1760 and the canal through the village was opened in 1798. By 1888 there was an annual total of almost 800,000 tons of cargo passing through the village on the canal. The railway arrived in 1841, causing a decline in popularity of canal-based transport through the valley.

100

TARRAN-NEWLAND HOUSES

for HALIFAX

Soon, a hundred Halifax families will be enjoying the modern comfort of the Tarran-Newland House — a factory-built house which can be erected quickly, thus effecting economy in skilled site labour, and which displays the artistic line and fine workmanship which belong to the best architecture of all generations.

TARRAN INDUSTRIES LTD
Public Works, Building and Civil Engineering Contractors, Specialists in Factory-made Building Units.

Left: 'Tarran' pre-fabricated houses were erected at various sites around Halifax, notably, Abbey Park as well as areas such as Mytholmroyd, Sowerby Bridge and Hebden Bridge. Although they were intended to be of a temporary nature, most of them are still in existence today.

Below: Foundation-stone-laying ceremonies were commonplace around a century ago. There was a huge amount of building work as a result of the development of public services of all descriptions, made possible by increasing wealth and employment. This picture really captures the spirit of the occasion, with a variety of totally natural expressions visible on the faces of the guests attending the ceremony. Each person blissfully unaware that their presence is being recorded for us to see almost 100 years later.

The foundation stone in question is being laid by Councillor Joseph Greenwood, Chairman of the Governors at the *Hebden Bridge United District Board School* - later to become Hebden Bridge Grammar School. The photograph was taken at 6.00pm on July 28th, 1908.

Right: The Royal Electric Theatre, a purpose-built early cinema located in Hebden Bridge. Few pictures survive of this, one of the district's earliest entertainment venues, known by many at the time as 'The Wooden Hut' or 'The Tub Hut'. Despite its ancient appearance the cinema was not the first to open in Hebden Bridge. That achievement belongs to 'Blake's Alhambra', a portable theatre which used to show early films on the Market Ground. The Picture House in Hebden Bridge was opened in July 1921.

The earliest 'moving pictures' to be shown in our district were probably those associated with travelling picture show companies which would set up marques on various fairground sites. The Electric Theatre at Exley was a very early form of cinema which began with the opening of *Halifax Zoo* in 1909.

Below: An atmospheric scene showing Market Street, Hebden Bridge at the turn of the century. Hebden Bridge grew and developed on the strength of the textile industry from its earliest beginnings as a crossing place in the valley bottom. The industrial revolution and the introduction of steam power made increased levels of mass production possible in the heart of the town which became a centre for the manufacture of fustian. Before this time much of the production of textiles took place in the farmsteads and cottages on the surrounding hillsides. The buildings featured in this photograph appear to have changed little in the space of almost a century. At the time of writing they are occupied by a variety of book shops, furniture retailers and businesses engaged in the tourist trade.

Above: An interesting turn of the century scene on a sunny day at the Hebden Bridge tram terminus. The off-set tram pole, which had the function of picking up the current from the overhead cables, and is a characteristic of these early vehicles, is clearly shown in this photograph. The atmosphere is enhanced by the delightful gas lamps and the abundance of pedestrians in the picture.

Above: A post-war scene outside Luddenden Post Office, with bunting displayed high above street level for some celebration or other. The Union Jack hanging from the window might indicate that the event in question was the Coronation of Queen Elizabeth II.

Below: It would be dangerous to pose for a photograph on this spot in modern times, for it is the busy junction of Burnley Road and New Road in Mytholmroyd. The picture features a very early tram, before similar vehicles were enclosed to protect the driver and passengers form the elements. The high wall on the left of the picture surrounds the grounds of Calder Grange, the victorian house which was demolished in the 1960s. The overhead tram cables, much less ornate than their counterparts nearer Halifax, can clearly be seen, as can the telegraph poles carrying the wires for the local telephone service.

Above: Electric tram services were introduced to Halifax and district in 1898. The area was one of the first in the country to be served by an electric tram system, at the time the only other Corporation-run systems were in Dover, Leeds and, not surprisingly, Blackpool. This photograph shows Car No. 94 standing at the terminus in Hebden Bridge with a similar vehicle behind it. At this time there were 94 vehicles of this type in use, all purchased before 1903. The Hebden Bridge route was the longest operated by Halifax Corporation and, as the destination board indicates, the journey took passengers via Cow Green. This is one of the early cars operated by the Authority; the open-topped vehicles had a short wheelbase and very narrow (3ft. 6in) gauge. The narrowness of the gauge, chosen because of the town's narrow streets and steep gradients, was to result in instability and cause several accidents over the 41 year tramway era in Halifax.

Right: A 1930s advert for a slightly more modern form of transport that eventually took over the role that trams had played in mass public transportation.

The Corporation and Joint Committee operate regular bus services to all parts of the Borough and to towns and rural districts beyond the Borough.

The transport area abounds in places of interest. Parks, Recreation Grounds, Public Libraries, Baths, etc., are generally not more than a 1½d. ride from the Town Centre. Places for Country Walks, Views from Hill Tops and Local Rambles lie further afield. There is a high frequency of service to most parts.

Official guides are issued gratis.

Dial 2718 Halifax for any further information.

Below: This picture is thought to date from the years shortly before the outbreak of the First World War. It was taken at Hardcastle Craggs, and readers familiar with the beauty spot will recognise the distinctive shape of the walls here; the track on the right now leads up to the car parking area.

The picture shows a remarkable number of passengers perched on top of the very sturdy cart, drawn by four equally robust white horses. It is likely that the people were part of an organised church outing or the like. Hardcastle Craggs attracted day trippers even in these times; often visitors would arrive in Hebden Bridge by train and be taken into the heart of Hardcastle Craggs by horse drawn vehicle. The horses appear slightly blurred in this picture; they obviously found it more difficult to keep still for the long exposure required than the straw-hatted party in the scene.

Below and right: Memories of Land Army girls in the Second World War; pictures taken in the Hebden Bridge area in the early 1940s. From May 1940, control over manpower, and woman power, rested in the hand of Ernest Bevin, the Minister of Labour. A report by Sir William Beveridge in December 1940 predicted that a million and a half women would be needed to assist with the war effort. This included all aspects of engineering and public services, as well as agriculture. From March 1941 the compulsory registration of women commenced. Eventually all women between the ages of 18 and 60 were registered. The war eliminated unemployment, and, by the end of 1941, 6 million workers were guaranteed jobs with decent minimum wages and conditions. For most, if not all women, war work was welcomed; 'good money' could be earned on a regular basis and the sense of purpose and camaraderie they experienced in the war years is looked back upon with fondness.

The introduction of the Women's Land Army repeated

> ## "RATIONING BEGAN IN 1940, INITIALLY ON BUTTER, SUGAR AND BACON"

an experiment that was first tried in the First World War. Britain, unlike Germany, was operating under a siege-economy with an unprecedented degree of state control and involvement in the daily lives of her citizens. In Germany rations were comparatively high, taxes relatively low and the female civilian population was never fully mobilized to help the war effort. Britain experienced severe shortages of imported fruit, especially bananas and oranges, and this would remain the case until well after the end of the conflict. Eggs were extremely scarce, either because the chickens had been eaten or because there was no grain to feed them with. Rationing began in January 1940, initially on butter, sugar and bacon. As the war progressed rationing was extended to cover other foodstuffs, meat in March 1941, and cheese in May the same year. Clothing too, was subject to tight controls and constant shortages. Against this background

80,000 members of the Women's Land Army set to work, many of them on Calderdale's farms and small holdings, to increase the production of much-needed rations for the nation. Parks and flower beds were ploughed up and vegetables were planted in them. 'Dig for Victory' was the theme as Britain sought ever more ingenious ways of feeding her population through the dark days of the war.

ACKNOWLEDGMENTS

THE PUBLISHERS WOULD
LIKE TO TO THANK THE
FOLLOWING FOR THEIR HELP
IN MAKING THIS BOOK
POSSIBLE

STEPHEN GEE

MAURICE JAGGER

GEOFF WHIPPEY

JOHN GREAVES

THE STAFF AT THE HALIFAX CENTRAL LIBRARY

ALBERT BERRY

MARGARET DUFFIELD

JACK UTTLEY

CALDERDALE METROPOLITAN BOROUGH

COUNCIL LEISURE SERVICES